# Cycling in
# The West Country

## Helen Stephenson

SIGMA
Leisure

**Published by** Sigma Leisure – an imprint of
Sigma Press, 1 South Oak Lane, Wilmslow, Cheshire SK9 6AR, England.

**British Library Cataloguing in Publication Data**
A CIP record for this book is available from the British Library.

**ISBN:** 1-85058-460-5

**Cover photograph:** Mid Devon Countryside (by kind permission of Mid Devon District Council)

**Photographs:** all photographs are by the author except for:
The Alfred Monument at Athelney, by Lotte Reider;
Cyclists 'dying by chocolate', by Gilly Freedman;
St Michael's Chapel, Burrow Mump, by Mark Hall.

**Maps:** L.S. Burford

**Typesetting and Design by:** Sigma Press, Wilmslow, Cheshire.

**Printed by:** MFP Design & Print

# Preface

The "West Country" to a Cornishman and Northumbrian may have different meanings. To the former, it may extend little further than the eastern boundary of Devon; to the latter, it may comprise a region encompassing Somerset, Avon, Devon, Cornwall, Dorset and, perhaps, parts of Wiltshire and Gloucestershire. For the purposes of this book, my "West Country" takes in Somerset and a good proportion of Devon since this is the "patch" that has been my backyard in recent years and which I have been exploring on two wheels whenever the opportunity has arisen. Fortunately I have been in a position to engineer many an opportunity.

While many associate Devon with quite intensive tourism and standstills on major 'A' roads at the height of the summer it is possible to be within five to ten miles of the busy holiday routes and encounter few vehicles other than those peculiar to the rural scene. The Blackdown Hills and East Devon Areas of Outstanding Natural Beauty offer the discerning cyclist exquisite views of tumbling wooded combes, distant ridges and Estuaries. Effort is always richly rewarded.

Mid Devon's enticements include a journey courtesy of Devon County Council's Bike Bus, rolling copsed hills, and hidden river valleys. From undulating ridges the cyclist can gaze at Dartmoor's highest tors, monitor the weather and observe the Moor's changing moods.

I consider Somerset to be the country's most varied county but would never have discovered its diversity without being persuaded to climb into the saddle. Which other county can proffer: golden sandy beaches, rugged precipitous cliffs, fossil laden slates, the open moorland of Exmoor, four ranges of hills with their own unique features (the Quantocks, Brendons, Blackdowns and Mendips). the rolling Isle Valley, the honey coloured hamstone villages and the Moors and Levels of central Somerset that constitute a wetland of international significance? I rest my case.

From the moment that Somerset revealed these hitherto hidden delights, the notion of providing cycling holidays came to mind. Once the need to reduce routes to paper for my then hypothetical customers arose, a book wasn't far behind.

The routes which I have selected are chosen to convey the diversity on offer in both Devon and Somerset, a diversity which is complemented by a network of untrafficked roads that is probably second to none. The total distance travelled on A roads is less than 10 miles for the totality of the routes; B roads are also kept to a minimum.

Although at either end of the spectrum there are routes of 12 to 15 miles and 50 to 60 miles the majority are in the region of 25 to 35, a comfortable day's cycling. This enables the absorption of places of interest, fine watering holes and tea rooms. Many of the routes have themes intended to convey a modest understanding of the history of my adopted home.

Sadly what should be a sane, sensible, stress free transport combination – train & bicycle – is not readily realised in the region. Friends and families are denied the opportunity of cycling and travelling by train together although some enlightened attitudes are emerging. Where a station can be incorporated in a route I have done so but most starting points assume (unless you are joining a route from home) the use of four wheels.

*Helen Stephenson*

# Contents

## SOMERSET

### *The Moors and Levels*

# West Somerset

# Exmoor

# DEVON
## East Devon

# Appendices

# Introduction

What follows is only the briefest introduction to the geography and history of the area covered by this book. A selected reading list appears in the bibliography on page 156.

## Geography and Geology

A brief scan of the 1:50,000 Ordnance Survey maps that cover this 'West Country' immediately reveals geographical variety from the limestone plateau of the Mendips in the east through the clay and peat 'Levels' in a central basin, the steeply-wooded combes of Quantocks and Brendons with their scattered small settlements, the Blackdown Hills with their densely afforested northern slopes to East Devon's pebble heaths and the apparent contradiction of Exmoor Forest.

This is a simplistic description and I leave the detailed geology to the experts. Suffice it to say that Devonian rocks, slates, sandstones and some limestones form the Brendons, Quantocks and Exmoor. Sluggish rivers cross the Liassic mud and peat Levels. The Blackdowns straddle the Devon-Somerset boundary and are covered almost entirely by Upper Greensand giving rise to poor acidic soils. Here, however, rise the Rivers Culm, Otter and Yarty which flow south and the Tone and Isle which flow north. There is also some chalk, and flints occur on the highest land.

Cycling provides an ideal opportunity to observe local building styles and materials. It will soon become apparent that the diversity of building stone offered up by the above is reflected in the character of the vernacular architecture. It is usually the more modest houses that illustrate local building styles and techniques; the larger houses of the eighteenth and nineteenth centuries often conform to fashionable tastes or incorporate imported materials. Look out for Blue Lias limestone and pantiles in the Polden Hills, flint churches in the Blackdowns and East Devon and the ubiquitous thatch and cob that appear across the region.

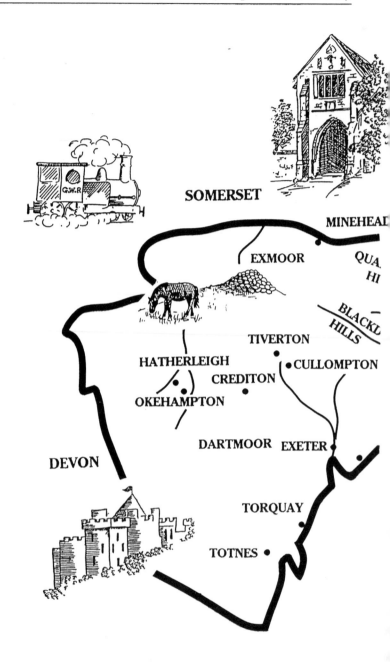

SOMERSET

MINEHEAD

EXMOOR

QUA
HI

BLACKL
HILLS

TIVERTON

HATHERLEIGH                    •CULLOMPTON

CREDITON

OKEHAMPTON

DARTMOOR  EXETER

DEVON

TORQUAY

TOTNES •

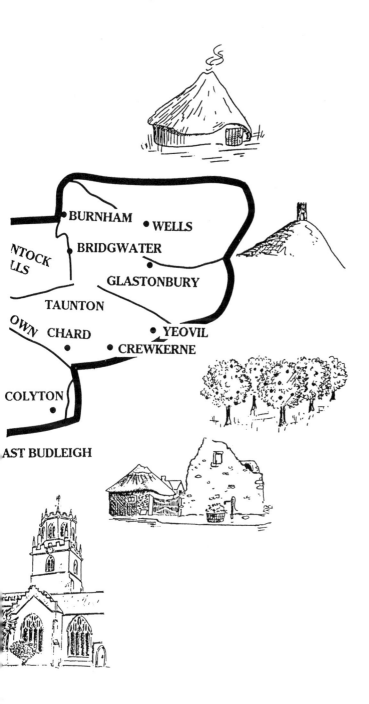

BURNHAM • WELLS

NTOCK
LLS

BRIDGWATER

GLASTONBURY

TAUNTON

OWN CHARD • YEOVIL
• CREWKERNE

COLYTON

AST BUDLEIGH

# Human Settlement

The region has long been settled. Neolithic farmers colonised the
Somerset Levels from around 3900 BC and built wooden trackways
including the Sweet Track, generally regarded as the world's oldest
man-made road. Its construction and that of subsequent tracks
illustrate management of woodland as a practice even 4000 years
ago. Hembury Fort, from which Broadhembury and Payhembury
take their names, is a prominent Iron Age fort but it was built over
a neolithic causewayed camp.

The Dumnonii were the British tribe that controlled the best part
of the Region. Geraint, defeated by Ine, the king of the West Saxons,
in AD 710 at Langport, was probably the last Dumnonian ' king'.

Although the Romans established themselves in Exeter and
much of the present day A30 represents the route of a Roman road,
evidence of occupation of this part of the South West is not particularly abundant.

Saxon 'invasion' (it is debatable whether the incursion from the
east was peaceful and a process of assimilation or a military con-
quest aimed at the extermination of the British) began in the fifth
century. There is an abundance of evidence of Saxon occupation.
Plentiful place names have their origins in old English both in
Somerset and Devon. Although Saxon churches were timber and
did not survive the sites of subsequent buildings are often those of
their English predecessors. Examples are Aller, North Curry, Wedmore, Stogumber and Shapwick.

The Normans left their castles which include Castle Neroche and
Bampton. Norman fonts survive, as does the fabric that housed
them. In addition to Medieval, Tudor and Elizabethan styles are
represented in the region.

# Trade and Industry

The clothing and woollen industries have played a particularly
important role in the wealth of the region. The villages on the River
Culm rose to prosperity in the fourteenth century. Commensurate
with this prosperity was the construction of particularly fine church
towers in Somerset and East Devon. Ports which no longer exist, e.g.
at Budleigh, once saw healthy activity as salt and other goods were

exported abroad. Carpet manufacture was established at Axminster at the tail end of the sixteenth century; the lace industry took a hold in Beer, Ottery St. Mary and Honiton.

High in the Blackdown Hills at Blackborough, workers from Cornwall formed the backbone of the whetstone industry. Quarrying of the excellent building stones, e.g. Ham Hill Stone (South Somerset) and Beer Stone, still contributes to the economy.

Farming and tourism form the mainstay of the region's economy today especially in Devon. Pastoral, arable and mixed agriculture are all practised. Although many acres of orchard have been grubbed up cider is still produced in respectable quantities in both counties. Perrys in Dowlish Wake, Sheppys in Taunton and Burrow Hill Cider, producers not only of cider but also Somerset Royal Cider Brandy, all provide the opportunity to taste West Country nectar!

# Literary Allusions

## R.D. Blackmore

The author of *Lorna Doone* was born in Berkshire but brought up in Culmstock, Devon. Although he is best known for the creation of the infamous Doone Clan and the hero Jan Ridd, Richard Doddridge Blackmore wrote a number of novels. Culmstock, Hemyock and Uffculme, three adjacent villages on the River Culm are represented in 'Perlycross' under the respective names of Perlycross, Perlycombe and Perliton. His father, the Reverend John Blackmore, was the vicar in Culmstock.

Old Blundells in Tiverton (now owned by the National Trust) was the school to which Jan Ridd was sent and where he fought Robin Snell.

## W.M. Thackeray

William Makepeace Thackeray spent vacations at Larkbeare to the north of Ottery St. Mary. Ottery is the Clavering St. Mary of his novel 'Pendennis'.

## S.T. Coleridge

The youngest of ten children of the Reverend John Coleridge and his second wife, Ann, Samuel Taylor Coleridge was born in Ottery St. Mary on 21st October 1772. Of a solitary disposition he was subjected to bullying in his childhood years. At the age of nine, following his father's death, he was sent to a boarding school in London. He made numerous visits home until a breakdown in his marriage led to a rift with his brothers which proved to be unbridgeable. He never visited Ottery again.

# Fable and Legend

I have not included a section on Arthur under **Human Settlement** because fable far exceeds fact. There seems little doubt that a British warrior by that name lived and died in the sixth century. He led the Britons against the Saxons in the major battle of Badon, reputedly at Solsbury Hill near Batheaston. The date of his death is variously recorded between 539 and 542 AD but not in the Anglo Saxon Chronicle which indicates it was not at the hands of the Saxons. This accords with the understanding that he met his death in a private quarrel arising in connection with his wife's reputation.

In any event as a Christian and great British general holding at bay a then heathen invading army of Saxons his memory is preserved in the Celtic folklore of Welsh, Cornish and Breton alike. For a fascinating analysis of the fact and fiction read the chapter, 'Arthur and Avalon' in Desmond Hawkin's book, 'Avalon and Sedgemoor'. For the purposes of 'Dark Peat, Watery Wastes and Arthurian Legend' allow reality and myth to merge.

The remoteness of the Blackdowns lends itself to the development of legend. Some of the Bronze Age barrows have been reputed to contain hidden treasure; stories are told of excavations being mysteriously closed overnight so that the more men laboured to retrieve lost hoards the more their goal was denied. Ride at dusk or in a mist along the Blackdown Ridge and the swaying of a branch or other shadowy movement excites the imagination. Reputed apparitions of headless horsemen or indeed the devil himself become quite credible; adrenalin flows.

# SOMERSET

## The Moors and Levels

# Ride 1

## *The Alfred Trail – or the Conquest of the Danes and the Conversion of Guthrum*

**Route:**      Athelney – Edington – Wedmore – Aller – Athelney

**Distance:**   20 miles or 48 miles (full circuit)

**Map:**        O.S. Landranger 1:50,000 Series, sheets 182 and 193

---

The full route is a circuit of approximately 48 miles but it can be conveniently divided into north and south sections. The route is described as a whole. If you choose the north or south section follow the amendments given at the end of the full directions.

The full route is covered by O.S. Landranger 1:50,000 Series, sheets 182 and 193. Sheet 182 covers the whole of the north section. Both Sheets are required for the south section.

◎ Start at the layby on the A361 near the Athelney Monument (Grid Reference 345294 Sheet 193, Taunton & Lyme Regis) which, surprisingly, given the significance of the location, is not accessible by public footpath.

Let your mind wander to the ninth century when the reedy marshes of these parts were more extensive. The discerning eye will notice that the monument is on slightly raised ground which the O.S. map dignifies as "Athelney Hill". Here, in 878, King Alfred was in temporary hiding from the Danes and was constructing a camp or fortress.

Guthrum, Arthur's foe, was at Chippenham where news would have reached him that the Danish leaders Hubbar and Ingar together with

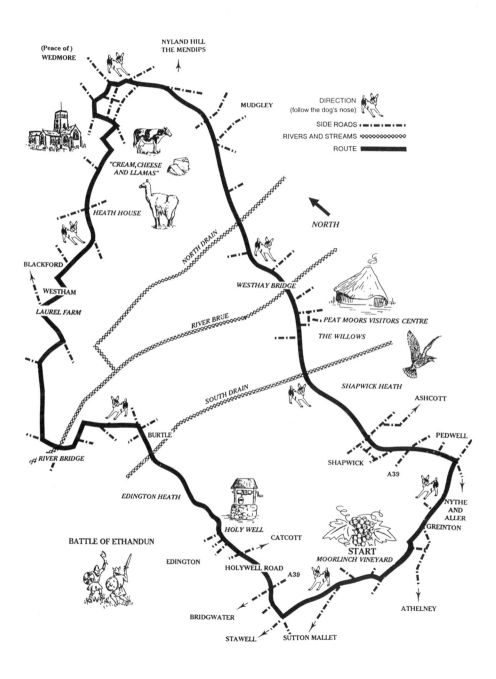

**The Alfred Monument, Athelney**

some 1200 men had been defeated by the English under the leadership of Odda*.

◎ Proceed north-eastwards for a mile or so over the Parrett, through Burrowbridge and round the corner to the "Mump". A quick sortie, on foot, to the top of the hill will find you puzzling over the "ruins" (genuine or 18th century folly?) of a chapel dedicated to St. Michael, patron saint of the Valley of the Parrett and the Brue.

The original chapel was a cruciform building belonging to Athelney Abbey which Alfred constructed as a Thanksgiving Abbey following the defeat of Guthrum and the Danes at Ethandun. But we have jumped too far ahead in the tale. For the present consider the Old English name for the Mump, Tutteyate or Tote Yate, suggesting a combination of "look-out" and "gateway". This is more representative of its function as part of Alfred's fortress.

◎ Retrace your steps to the River Parrett at Burrowbridge and turn right immediately before the river to follow the north bank to Moorland Farm (two 90 degree bends *en route*). After you have crossed the 'rhine' (local dialect for watercourse), turn right then left and follow this lane to meet the A371 At Double Bridge. Turn left and after approximately one third of a mile turn right. One and a half miles on you will be in Chedzoy. Pause at the Church to inspect the "tumble gate" or tumble-down stile in the north-west corner of the churchyard. From a distance the gate appears to be a fence, but closer examination reveals otherwise.

◎ Proceed eastwards through Parchey and over the King's Sedgemoor Drain then turn left towards Stawell (at the right time of year, from August to October, an amazing selection of English apples is available from the fruit farm).

---

* This brief account by the author represents her understanding of the argument put forward in W.H.P. Greswell's, "Dunmonia and the Valley of the Parrett".

**St Michael's Chapel, Burrow Mump**

◎ **After the church,** take the left turn which passes through an orchard as your first climb begins. Ignore the first lane to the left. At the next junction turn left for a short sharp rise to the A39. Cross this busy road with care to sail downhill, with marvellous Mendip views, towards Edington. This is Holywell Road which continues over the next crossroads and passes the Church of St. George before bending sharply to the right. Just before a left-hand bend is Edington's Holy Well, one of a number of Polden Village wells springing from the clays of the Lower Lias, a source of medicinal salts and, sometimes, of sulphuretted hydrogen. Certainly the well can be located by its odour from close to.

Now is the time to turn to the year 878, mindful of Alfred and forces from Somerset, Hampshire, Dorset and Wiltshire, engaging in encounters with the Danes. Taking the less orthodox "Somerset" view Alfred rendezvoused with the aforementioned forces to defeat the Danes, lead by Guthrum, at Ethandun (Edington Polden). Less controversial (the more orthodox view claims Edington, Wiltshire as the location of this decisive engagement) are the succeeding events.

◎ Continue north across Edington Heath, a peaty moor, to Burtle passing the Tom Mogg Inn on the left. Turn left immediately after the Church of St. Philip and St. James and continue to River Bridge. Turn right across the River Brue and, very shortly, right again for more level pedalling with the Mendip ridge in the distance. As yet the Isle of Wedmore is not apparent. At the next junction turn right then left and, at Laurel Farm, right through Westham. Ignore the first left turn and, a few hundred yards on, turn left to climb gently up past the Methodist Chapel of Heath House and continue ahead at the crossroads. Look out for Walnut Tree Farm, home to cream, cheese and llamas!

◎ You approach Wedmore village along Plud Street. Find your
  way to the Parish Church of St. Mary.

It is reasonably certain that there was, at least as early as the time
of Alfred, a church on more or less the same site. Here in Wedmore
Alfred concluded his peace with Guthrum and, following the latter's
baptism at Aller (more of which anon), at the Royal Villa, Guthrum
put off his white baptismal robe in the ceremony of Chrism-loosing.

The traditional site of Alfred's Palace is about half way up Mudgeley
Hill in a field called Court Garden.

◎ From St. Mary's Church, follow the B3151 in the direction of
  Glastonbury but NOT before visiting the interior.

Above the pulpit is an ancient mural painting of St. Christopher
carrying the Christ. There are three paintings imposed one upon the
other. It isn't possible to date the earliest picture but the latest is said
to date from circa 1520 and the one before that circa 1460. The lower
part of the picture shows in great detail ships, mermaids and fishes
signifying the earliest inundation of the moors by waters giving rise
to the description, "Isle of Wedmore".

◎ A slight rise out of the village gives way to a level mile
  bestowing dramatic views over Wedmore Moor to Nyland Hill
  and the Mendips beyond. There follows an exhilarating descent – down Mudgeley Hill with the moors beckoning and
  the Poldens to the south.

◎ Prevailing wind permitting, you sail southwards across North
  Drain and the black peat moors to cross the River Brue at
  Westhay. Follow the Shapwick (Peat Moors Visitor Centre)
  signs and you will soon pass the Visitor Centre and The
  Willows. Take the opportunity to explore the reconstructed
  settlement and trackways and to sample the irresistible con-
  fectionery offered by the tea room.

◎ From here the route continues in a southwesterly/southerly
  direction across South Drain (a continuation of the man-
  made Huntspill River) and Shapwick Heath.

The Nature Conservancy Council Reserve on this Heath has out-standing botanical interest containing a number of rarities. It is also a valuable breeding ground for such birds as nightingale, willow-tit, grasshopper-warbler and nightjar. (Binoculars would not be wasted on this route.)

◎ As you approach the village of Shapwick you experience the long since forgotten effort of an ascent. Pass the Shapwick House Hotel and the Church of St. Mary. Go straight ahead at the crossroads and follow the lane round to the left and up to meet the A39. Cross the main road to descend Pedwell Hill for just under a mile. Turn right onto the A361 then, almost immediately left onto a lane signposted to Nythe to continue your southerly journey.

In the winter of 1993/4 this road was flooded as were the surround-ing Butleigh Moor and King's Sedge Moor which resembled an inland lake.

◎ Cross Eighteen Feet Rhine then King's Sedgemoor Drain half a mile after which turn right. Enjoy a further level mile before a choice is to be made. If you turn right your way remains level. A dog leg bend to the left will bring you to the A372 onto which you turn left – shortly to arrive in Aller. But you will have missed the chance of yet another glorious view, possibly back over the 4 – 5 miles to the Polden Ridge. To avoid such a loss your route takes you left up to the wooded limestone Turn Hill which belongs to the National Trust. A further steeper left turn brings you to the entrance to the N T property. Enjoy! You will now have to retrace your steps to the last junction. From here turn left to descend through Beer and join the A372. Turn left again and (after about a mile and a half) you come to Aller. Turn right by The Old Pound Inn. The church is approached from the next turning on the left.

Standing on the low hill which is occupied by St. Andrew's Church one enjoys a rare and precious tranquillity. Aller means alder trees or shrubs and the first church was probably a Saxon wooden building with its altar placed on the baptismal site. Here Guthrum was baptised although the site's choice is a little baffling. Alfred may have distrusted the Danish leader and been unwilling to show him Athelney. Certainly a ceremony outside the church could have been attended and witnessed by large numbers.

◎ To return to Athelney, retrace your "steps" to the last junction and turn left to cross between North Moor and Aller Moor over the Sowy River to Pathe. Turn left and follow this lane up to the A361. Another left turn and you are 1.5 – 2 miles from Athelney. You may wish to dash up Burrow Mump again just to review your sojourn!

It was following the Peace of Wedmore that Alfred had Athelney Abbey constructed.

◎ *To begin the north section of this route:* visit Moorlynch Vineyard with a view to partaking of fine English Wine; use the prospect as a reward! Cycle right and down from the Vineyard to the junction. Turn right for a short rise past the church. At the junction bear left and then take the first right which is not very distinctive. You climb a little before cycling on the level to a crossroads at which you turn right for a sharp rise to the A39. You have now joined the main route. See paragraph 7 of the main text.

◎ To finish the north section and return to the Vineyard, instead of taking the turning to Nythe after descending Pedwell Hill continue along the A361 for about a mile taking the second right signposted Moorlinch. A right turn at the next junction will bring you into the village. Follow the road round to the right past the pub and up. Take the right turn to the Vineyard.

◎ To begin the south section visit Moorlynch Vineyard as above. Having cycled down to the junction turn left and follow the road round to the left, past the Ring Of Bells pub. Turn left at the next junction and, when you meet the A361, turn left to cycle for about a mile on this main road. Take the next turning on the right signposted Nythe. You are now back on the main route heading towards Aller via Turn Hill and Beer.

◎ To finish the south section and return to the Vineyard after you have passed the church in Stawell go straight ahead at the crossroads towards Moorlinch. Follow the lane into the village taking the left turn to the Vineyard.

# Ride 2

## *Dark Peat, Watery Wastes and Arthurian Legend*

**Route:**      East Huntspill – Godney – Glastonbury – Meare – Burtle
                – East Huntspill

**Distance:**   30 miles

**Map:**        O.S. Landranger 1:50,000 Series Sheet 181, Minehead &
                Brendon Hills area

---

At the beginning of this route of about 30 miles the Iron Age fortification of Brent Knoll commands the attention. Thereafter Glastonbury Tor is almost inescapable.

◎ Start at Secret World, New Road Farm, not far from High-bridge (Grid Reference 328456; O.S. Landranger 1:50,000 Series Sheet 182, Weston-super-Mare & Bridgwater area). From New Road Farm turn right to cycle east for one mile to meet the B3141 at East Huntspill. Turn right, pass the Inn and shop and take the next left towards Burtle.

The lane runs parallel to the River Huntspill but hedges obscure any sight of this man-made watercourse. A succession of River Catchment Boards had contemplated such a cut but it took the momentum of war to bring its construction into being and for the finance to be forthcoming. 3.5 million gallons of water per day were needed by the new munitions factory at Puriton.

◎ Go straight ahead at Cote Corner. When you reach the T-junction turn left and after about half a mile the road takes

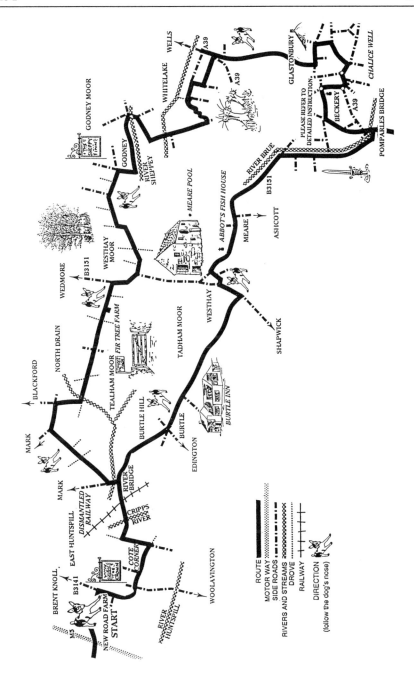

a 90 degree bend to head east. You soon cross the Cripps River and the route of the former Somerset and Dorset Railway.

(The line from Highbridge to Glastonbury was launched by Somerset and Dorset's predecessor, the Somerset Central Railway Company, founding directors of which were Cyrus and James Clark, also founders of the footwear industry.)

◎ Having crossed the Brue over River Bridge turn right along a sheltered lane that continues across Mark Moor. At the T-junction turn right to begin to sail across Tealham and Tadham Moors with a prevailing westerly wind behind you. Successive right and "left" turns take you across North Drain for a blissful open stretch in top gear.

Far fewer hedges align the watercourses here. To the north is the Isle of Wedmore, once surrounded by sea. The Somerset Trust For Nature Conservation manages a leased nature reserve at Tealham Moor.

◎ Go past the Pets Hotel at Fir Tree Farm and at the T-junction turn right onto the B3151 which bends sharply left then right. At this second bend cycle straight on towards Godney.

Peat asserts itself in this area. Commercial working of this "mineral" began in 1870 when it was sold for fuel, or as litter for livestock. Now a much mechanised industry, handwork is still needed to build up the peat into the drying positions which are a familiar part of the landscape. Peat is cut into cubes ("Humps") which are still wet. After drying for a few days the turfs are put into the smaller "stooks" or "hiles" which allow for the shrinkage of the blocks as they dry and then into the large "ruckles" in which they complete their drying.

◎ After passing two droves on the left, the road bends to the north then "dog legs" to the east. Cycling this stretch you will see the wooded Westhay Heath with its stands of silver birch. This is another S.T.N.C. Reserve.

◎ Another succession of droves and you turn right at a cross-roads to head south to Lower Godney and the Sheppey Inn. At the next crossroads turn right over the sleepy Sheppey to double back on yourself for about half a mile. (If you had a tail wind heading east you'll know about it now!!). Just before another severe bend look up to the right to the Chapel, accessed by a private track.

The Church of the Holy Trinity was rebuilt in 1839 on the site of an ancient Chapel recorded on some of the country's earliest charters.

◎ Cross the Whitelake River and turn left at the next junction for a wonderful weaving willow-lined lane where speed is NOT of the essence.

Indeed, the camber of this road precludes haste. This can only be Somerset. When pollarded severely the form of the trees can wreak havoc with the imagination, especially if visualised as truncated limbs.

◎ Where a track leads north across an old bridge the road turns sharply right. Cycle parallel to the Whitelake for a couple of hundred yards before turning right and then left to the A39. Turn right and take the next left for the unfamiliar feeling of an ascent and a steep one at that as Edmund Hill beckons you towards the Tor and St. Michael's Tower.

◎ Go over the brow of the hill and over a crossroads (residential). Where the road bends to the right turn left. In front of you is a wonderful thatched house. This lane, Wick Hollow, takes you under a majestic canopy which forms the leafy ceiling of a cutting. Tree roots, exposed for some years, drop down from on high and ensure the diversion of your attention from the gradient. Continue up the Hollow, ignoring lanes on left and right. As you approach a T-junction the Tor reveals itself. Turn left at the junction. You will quickly see the path that leads up the north side of the Tor to the tower, once part of a chapel built around 1330 which replaced a Norman Chapel thrown down by an earthquake in 1275.

The tower is battlemented and has an interesting relief of St. Bridgit (who is reputed to have come over from Ireland on a pilgrimage to the town in 488 AD.) milking a cow. This spot is forever stained with the blood of Thomas Whiting, the last Abbot of Glastonbury who was hung and then drawn and quartered.

◎ To return to the town turn left from the start of the footpath and go straight down the hill exercising great care: the lane is steep and, from April to September, we are likely to encounter vehicular congestion at weekends. At the foot of the hill a right turn onto the A361 is required. Descend the hill. At the first roundabout turn left, at the second go straight ahead. The Abbey is on your right, behind a car park and the Town Hall.

Here, according to legend, lie King Arthur and Queen Guinevere. You will discover the many legends that abound as you explore the town's shops. Mystery and myth apart, in its heyday, Glastonbury housed Britain's oldest church and the first Christian Altar. The Abbey must have been one of the wonders of the Middle Ages.

◎ To return westwards, take the first left turn (Benedict Street) at the roundabout in the lower part of the town, to cycle past St. Benedict's Church, built by Abbot Richard Bere around 1500. You are now approaching Glastonbury's industrial quarter with its timber and building yards.

◎ At the crossroads go left through Beckery — not the most picturesque of locations but nevertheless inextricably linked with the romances of King Arthur and once housing the "Chapel Adventurous" about which the King once dreamed. Follow the road down to meet the A39 as it crosses Pompar- les Bridge, a structure once recorded as "a Bridge of Stone of four arches communely Pontperlus where men fable that Arture cast in his swerd". Having crossed the Brue turn immediately right to follow the left bank northwards to meet the B3151 at Cold Harbour Bridge. Turn left and head for Meare with caution as this road can be busy.

◎ As you approach Meare, another "island" in times gone by, you will see, on the right, the Abbot's Fish House".

This reflects the existence of important fisheries and expansion of freshwater in the 14th century. The Abbot's Manor House was built and improved in the period 1323-1524 by successive abbots of Glastonbury.

The O.S. map shows "Meare Pool" directly to the north of the Church. The village takes its name from the meres or lakes which once surrounded it and which were of a considerable size. The Lake Village of Meare flourished from about 250 B.C. on the verge of such a lake.

Some of the earliest man-made wooden roadways have been discovered in the vicinity. These include the Abbott's Way which linked Meare to Burtle, and was constructed of a line of split alder trees, and the late Bronze Age Meare Heath Trackway.

◎ Continue through Oxenpill towards Westhay. Take the Shapwick/Burtle turning and turn left at the next junction. Take the next right across Westhay Heath to Burtle (and the Burtle Inn). Burtle Hill — well, against the wind it's as good as an incline and to be fair there is a slight gradient — takes you towards River Bridge. From here retrace your steps to New Road Farm.

# Ride 3

## *A Trip Back in Time*

**Route:**      East Huntspill – Rooks Bridge – Brent Knoll –
                East Huntspill

**Distance:**   12 miles

**Map:**        O.S. Landranger 1:50,000 Series Sheet 182.

---

◎ Start at Secret World, New Road Farm (Grid Reference
  328456; O.S. Landranger 1:50,000 Series Sheet 182,
  Weston-super-Mare & Bridgwater area). Turn right out of
  New Road Farm and cycle to the end of the road. Turn left to
  cross over the River Brue and cycle through Bason Bridge
  with its creamery.

Undistinguished now, Bason Bridge once had its own station on the
original Somerset Central line out of Highbridge which at the turn
of the century had the county's largest dairy market.

◎ At the next junction go right onto the B3139 (signposted
  Wedmore and Wells). Pass the woodcraft work and show-
  rooms, windmill and the Watchfield Inn. Take the second
  road on the left (Dutch Road), cycle past Dutch Road Farm
  and Dutch Court Farm. Turn right at the T-junction then
  immediately left.

◎ Three-quarters of a mile on, at a junction, follow the road that
  swings round to the left to run northwards over land that in
  all probability is below sea level.

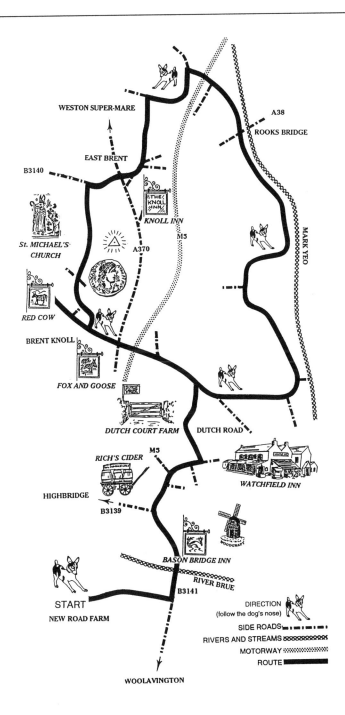

WESTON SUPER-MARE

A38
ROOKS BRIDGE

EAST BRENT

B3140

THE KNOLL INN

KNOLL INN

MARK YEO

St. MICHAEL'S CHURCH

A370

M5

RED COW

BRENT KNOLL

FOX AND GOOSE

DUTCH COURT FARM    DUTCH ROAD

RICH'S CIDER    M5

WATCHFIELD INN

HIGHBRIDGE

B3139

WOODCRAFT

BASON BRIDGE INN

RIVER BRUE

START    B3141

NEW ROAD FARM

DIRECTION
(follow the dog's nose)

SIDE ROADS
RIVERS AND STREAMS
MOTORWAY
ROUTE

WOOLAVINGTON

◎ Continue northwards. The road dog-legs left, right and left
   again to pick up the Mark Yeo.

This modest stream, created as the Pillrow Cut by medieval monks
from Glastonbury, connects the Rivers Brue and Axe and gave the
town an excellent access route to the sea. In medieval England
Glastonbury was an important seafaring centre; the Mark Yeo was
the first major artificial waterway on the Somerset Levels.

◎ At Rooks Bridge cross the A38.

Here, a few houses scattered on either side of the road tell little of
the past yet this was home to mill and port facilities for loading and
unloading the boats that came alongside wharfs to put goods ashore
or transfer their cargoes into smaller vessels bound for Glastonbury.
The waterway you see today, much reduced in size, once formed a
principal transport route between Glastonbury and its coastal es-
tates at Brent and Berrow. Imagine a channel with sufficient capacity
to transport 1500 seats for the church of St. Johns from Bristol to
Glastonbury via Rooks Mill.

◎ After just over half a mile turn right to cross the M5 then left
   and left again to arrive at East Brent, once part of the
   Glastonbury Estate, deep in the Brent Marshes, as Avalon
   was once known.

As you approach the A370, parched thirsts can be quenched at The
Knoll Inn.

◎ Turn right onto the main road then almost immediately left
   onto the B3140 which traces an arc around the northern edge
   of the Iron Age Hill Fort of Brent Knoll. (This fortification is
   best appreciated from the top, reached by a number of
   paths.) The road swings right. Ignore the turn signed 'Church'
   and the next (a cul-de-sac). Take the following lane on the
   left and climb from sea level to all of 50 metres to sail down
   towards the village of Brent Knoll (formerly South Brent).

Take time to visit St. Michael's Church, constructed of lias and freestone in the decorated and perpendicular style. Look for the finely carved bench ends that depict the medieval legend of an abbot who came to despoil the clergy of South Brent. He is represented by a fox and the clergy, who have him hung, as geese.

◎ From the church follow the signed path to the summit of the Knoll to discover the remains of a camp with a double fosse.

Roman coins have been found here and, probably at Battleborough, the Britons fought off a Danish advance. Consider this as you watch the motorway meander interminably into the distance.

◎ Return to the church and, if liquid refreshment is required, repair to the Red Cow. To reach this pub turn right from the church then left to meet the lane that completes the arc around the Knoll. Turn right and the Red Cow is about 400 yards along on the right. To return to New Road Farm, turn left from the pub and continue to the junction with the A38. Cross this busy road, pass the Fox and Goose and proceed over the motorway. About a mile from the motorway bridge, turn right (you will have passed Somerset Court and Chelsea Farm) to retrace your 'steps' past Dutch Court Farm.

◎ Turn right onto the B3139 and return to New Road Farm via Bason Bridge.

# Ride 4

## *The Willow Trail (Secret World, New Road Farm, East Huntspill to Mark & back)*

**Route:**  East Huntspill – Mark – East Huntspill

**Distance:**  13 miles.

**Map:**  O.S. Landranger 1:50,000 Series Sheet 182.

Although we are in the land of the willow tree, on the edge of Somerset's Moors and Levels, this route takes its name not from the tree but one of the badgers at New Road Farm. To learn more about Willow pay a visit to this working farm and animal centre. The Farm's Interpretation Centre is an excellent place to learn the history of man's interminable battle against water inundation in this region and about the willow industry.

The route is 13 miles long and an easy and enjoyable way to gain a feel for the atmosphere of the remarkably horizontal landscape. Huntspill Level appears to enjoy a high point of five feet above sea level. Huntspill and Mark Moors, over which you cycle, are partly below sea level.

◎ Start at New Road Farm (Grid Reference 328456; O.S. Landranger 1:50,000 Series Sheet 182, Weston-super-Mare & Bridgwater area). Turn right from the Farm and, after a mile turn right onto the B3141. Follow the B road through East Huntspill past the Inn and shop. Where it bends sharply to the right (about a quarter of a mile from the Inn) take the "left" turn signposted "Burtle".

◎ At the next T-junction the main route takes you left. A diver-

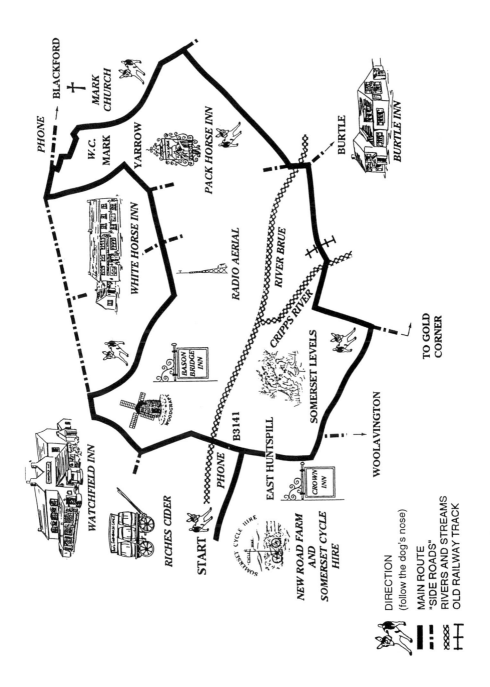

BLACKFORD

PHONE →

MARK CHURCH

PHONE

W.C. MARK

YARROW

PACK HORSE INN

WHITE HORSE INN

RADIO AERIAL

RIVER BRUE

BURTLE

BURTLE INN

CRIPPS RIVER

BASON BRIDGE INN

WOODGRAY

SOMERSET LEVELS

TO GOLD CORNER

WATCHFIELD INN

RICHES CIDER

START

B3141

PHONE

EAST HUNTSPILL

CROWN INN

WOOLAVINGTON

NEW ROAD FARM AND SOMERSET CYCLE HIRE

SOMERSET CYCLE HIRE

DIRECTION
(follow the dog's nose)

MAIN ROUTE
"SIDE ROADS"
RIVERS AND STREAMS
OLD RAILWAY TRACK

sion to the right will take you a short distance along the Huntspill River to Gold Corner, the National Rivers Authority's largest Pumping Station on the Levels. Take time to note the highest recorded water level then retrace your steps to the junction where you turned right. To rejoin the main route go straight on.

◎ Continue northwards and round a ninety degree bend to cross the Cripps River and a raised bank that represents the last remains of the Somerset & Dorset railway line that ran from Highbridge to Glastonbury. At the next junction (River Bridge) turn left over the Brue then take the first right turn, about two hundred yards further on.

◎ Cycle along this hedged lane that gives you views of the Mendip Hills, over the Mark Yeo (merely a small stream) and, at the T-junction, turn left. Cross the Shipham Rhyne and meander into Mark passing the church as you emerge into the village.

The Parish church is guarded by lions and seems disproportionately large. It is worth a visit not least because it represents some nine hundred years of history.

◎ Turn left onto the B3139 to pass the Pack Horse on your left (or not as the case may be – open fires and budgerigars are on offer). A quarter of a mile further on, as you approach another ninety degree bend, the White Horse faces you.

An extensive menu including sumptuous desserts and an impressive selection of Real Ales greet the patron of this establishment.

◎ Follow that ninety degree bend round to the left then take the lane that goes straight on to follow the Mark Yeo through Yarrow.

You may find a stall outside one of the houses down here with homemade preserves and chutneys for sale.

◎ Another sharp bend obliges you to turn right. Go straight ahead at the next junction and straight on at the following crossroads. This lane brings you round, through Southwick (a few houses either side of the road) to the B3141 at Watchfield.

◎ Turn left onto the B road to head towards Bason Bridge and back to East Huntspill. *En route* you pass the Watchfield Inn and a windmill where a woodcraft work and showroom is based. About three-quarters of a mile after you cross the River Brue is the right turn that takes you back to New Road Farm.

**A rural byway: perfect for cycling!**

# South Somerset

# Ride 5

## *Bloody Rebellion*

**Route:**      Ilminster – Stocklinch – Barrington – Puckington –
                Hatch Beauchamp – Bickenhall – Ilminster

**Distance:**   35 miles.

**Map:**        O.S. Landranger 1:50,000 Series Sheet 193.

---

This route of approximately 35 miles starts from Ditton Street Car
Park in Ilminster (The Principal Route). It includes Barrington
Court, the Elizabethan Mansion owned by the National Trust. An
alternative starting point, closer to Taunton, is the layby at Henlade,
just under two miles south-east of junction 25 on the M5, on the
A358.

## Principal Route

◉ Begin at the car park in Ditton Street (Grid Reference 362145;
O.S. Landranger 1:50,000 Series Sheet 193, Taunton &
Lyme Regis). Turn right towards the town centre and at the
crossroads **(Market Square, \*; see alternative route, below)** go right, up the hill to pick up the main road. Turn right
onto this road which, after a couple of hundred yards, bears
left.

To the left are the grounds of Dillington House now owned by
Somerset County Council and run as an adult education centre: it
was formerly owned by the Speke family of whom more anon.

◉ Cycle along the southern boundary of the grounds and after

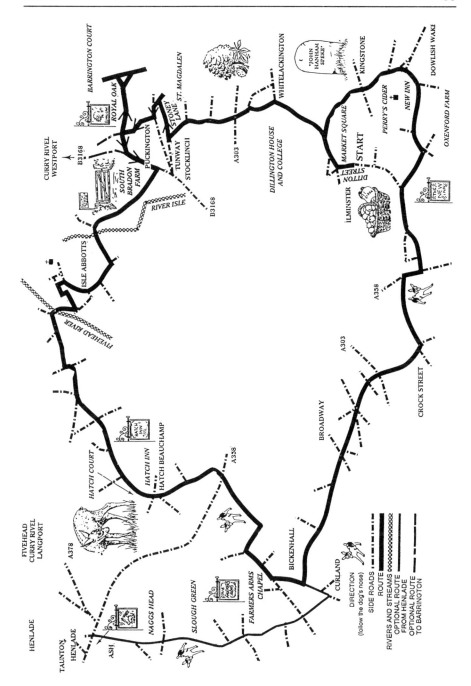

a gate-house on your left turn sharply left towards Stocklinch.

On the opposite side from this turning lies Whitelackington with its 17th house and church. The garden to the house once boasted a horse chestnut tree where the crowds gathered to see James, Duke of Monmouth during the course of his visit to the Speke family in 1680.

◎ The lane to Stocklinch crosses the A303 and bends successively right, left, right and left.

This village of no shops nevertheless possesses two churches. After the last left bend you come to Stocklinch St. Magdalen on your right. This small church has a peculiar charm with its external bells and should be paid a visit.

◎ Return to the lane through the village and, at the T-junction,
   turn right into Stoney Lane to climb steeply past picturesque
   cottages to your left. At the top of the rise turn left then left
   again. At the next junction turn right down a lovely lane laden
   with wayside vegetation. At the bottom take another right turn
   to the church with its octagonal tower and the Royal Oak
   which offers the thirsty rider real ales, continental beers and
   country wines.

◎ To find the Court continue past the pub to the eastern end of
   the village where you bear left.

The Court, which dates from about 1570, has gardens laid out by Gertrude Jeckyll and is now owned by the National Trust. The mansion is of Ham Stone, bears the signs of the Ham Hill masons and is laid out in an "E" shape. *En route* to or from the Court you will note that the village has more than its fair share of golden thatched cottages, several dating back to the Middle Ages.

◎ Return through the village to its western end and turn left onto
   the B3168 to climb gently into Puckington. Just before the
   telephone box turn right The lane meets the River Isle at

South Bradon Farm and continues in a north easterly direction to cross it. Turn right at the T-junction towards Isle Abbotts whose church tower is one of three in Somerset together described as "among the great masterpieces of English Architecture".

'Isle' does not mean island. It has its origins in the Celtic name, Gifl, for the River Yeo.

◎ From the church gate cycle straight ahead then turn right and almost immediately left. At the next junction turn right. This takes you over the Fivehead River, a tributary of the Isle and supplier of water to an essentially arable area. At the next junction turn left to Curry Mallett (another village associated with the Speke family), and from there follow the signs to Hatch Beauchamp.

The road linking these two villages passes Hatch Court and its park. Almost certainly you will come across a herd of Fallow deer browsing under the oak trees. June sees the birth of the fawns, spotted like the adults in their summer coats. The court is open to the public for a limited period.

◎ When you reach the T-junction (opposite the Hatch Inn) turn right then immediately left. Pass the 18th century Inn on your left and Beauchamp House on your right. Follow Village Road down to meet the A358 and turn right then immediately left for a steady climb to Bickenhall.

This, however, is Somerset and to divert your attention from the effort the hedgerows present a variety of wildflowers and hedgerow species: honeysuckle, hazel, dog rose and oak in the hedges themselves while, in, June, attendant upon them are cow parsley, yellow and purple vetches, speedwell, herb robert, bedstraws and meadowsweet.

◎ After about a mile turn left. Take the second turning on the left towards Curland (just beyond the chapel on your right).

A further left turn brings a short-lived rise onto a wonderfully gentle rolling ridge road that carries you towards Broadway and the Isle Valley.

Many of the roads in the region run remarkably straight. Don't be deceived into thinking them to be Roman; they are routes laid out when the former Common land was parcelled out. The village takes its name from the "Broad Way" which led to the medieval forest of Neroche and once formed an ancient roadway between the Iron Age hillforts of Ham Hill and Castle Neroche.

Don't get too carried away on this glorious high-gear "highway" or you may miss the opportunity to investigate Jacob Spinners, where a mixed herd of Jacob, Dorset and Shetland sheep are reared, their wool spun and sweaters produced. Customers return demanding garments from the wool of 'their' sheep.

◎ This route does not take you into the village of Broadway. Rather, you cycle through a four lane crossroads and arrive at a five lane crossroads. The Five Dials pub is just downhill to your left. You are now in Horton (once, along with Broadway afforested and part of the Royal Forest). Go straight ahead along Pottery Lane to Crock Street passing under the A303. You have to exert some effort to reach this settlement where a left turn gives a deserved descent to the A358. Turn right then left towards Ilminster.

The character of the area has changed; we are now in the catchment of the River Isle.

◎ A mile on the level brings you to a right turn (signposted Cricket Malherbie) and a short climb (examine those hedgerows!). At the top of the hill is a crossroads at which you turn left to pick up the South Somerset Cycle Route. At Oxenford Farm keep right and follow the lane down into Dowlish Wake for liquid refreshment at The New Inn or Perry's Cider if your thirst demands some Somerset Nectar.

Duly fed and watered, take some time to appreciate a particularly picturesque hamstone hamlet which dates to at least Norman times. We are once again in the territory of the Speke family. John Hanning Speke (discoverer of the source of the Nile) is buried in the church together with other members of a distinguished dynasty.

◉ Return to Ilminster by continuing north from the church to a T-junction. Turn right then almost immediately left to descend to the Minster on the Isle.

A small diversion to the right will bring you to Kingstone Church which appears quite disproportionate in grandeur to the area it seems to serve.

◉ Alternative route: from Henlade

◉ Turn left from the layby at Henlade (Grid Reference 276237; O.S. Sheet 193) to brave the dual carriageway to the first crossroads, at the foot of the hill before the traffic lights, and turn right with care. Pass the pub and then Ash Hill Caravan and Camping site. Climb gently up ignoring turns to Stoke St. Mary and West Hatch towards and through Slough Green. Ignore the sign to the Farmers Arms! Cycle to the next crossroads and go straight ahead to Curland. Here turn left and take the second right to bring you onto the 'broadway'. You have now joined the Principal Route.

◉ When you reach Ilminster pick up the Principal Route from the Market Square, marked with an asterisk, *.

◉ To return to Henlade instead of turning left past the Hatch Inn at Hatch Beauchamp turn right. Follow this lane for a mile and a half to meet the A358 onto which you turn right. After another mile and a half you will see the layby on the right.

# Notes

## Ilminster

For a detailed history of the town up to the beginning of this century, James Street's 'The Mynster of the Ile' is highly recommended.

Ilminster is recorded at Domesday and a church has stood on the site since Saxon times. The Romans were well settled in the district holding British inhabitants in subjection until forced to flee before Saxon invaders about AD 440. The great Roman road or Fosse Way is now represented by the A303 from Ilchester to South Petherton thence the road through Lopen to Dinnington.

Domesday brought into Ilminster the Forest of Neroche, one of the five royal forests of the county. "Forest" means an extensive territory of uncultivated ground kept in virgin condition for the wild "beasts of the forest", "beasts of chase" and "beasts and fowls of warren". These respectively are hart, hind, hare, boar and wolf; buck, doe, fox, marten and foe; hare, rabbit, pheasant and partridge.

A selection of good tea shops apart, the town boasts a fine market square and a grammar school dating from 1586.

## Hatch Court

Opening times: House and gardens – Thursday afternoons, mid-June to mid-September 2.30 – 5.30 (last admission 5pm); Gardens only – Friday afternoons, early June to end of September 2.30 – 5.30.

# Ride 6

## *The Blackdown Ridge – Border Country*

**Route:**  Taunton/Trull – Daws Green – Millhayes – Culmstock –
Hemyock  –  Churchinford  –  Blagdon  Hill  –
Trull/Taunton

**Distance:**  25 miles.

**Map:**  O.S. Landranger 1:50,000 Series Sheet 193.

---

◎ This route of 25 miles meanders up the northern slopes of an
Area of Outstanding Natural Beauty, dips into the Culm valley
to visit an antiquity and church of special interest before
climbing gently to a wonderful watering hole then dropping
back down to the starting point.

◎ You cannot escape gradients when crossing the Blackdowns
but you can sneak up onto the top avoiding the "arrows" and
the rewards for one's efforts are tremendous.

◎ The route starts in Trull opposite the Post Office on Church
Road at the junction with Trull Road, the 'main' road south
from Taunton through Trull and Blagdon Hill (Grid Reference
213223; O.S. 1:50,000 Landranger Series Sheet 193, Taunton & Lyme Regis). Turn right onto Trull Road then immediately left towards Dipford.

◎ Keep straight on until you reach a fork at Dipford; bear right
and climb gently towards Daw's Green. At Daw's Green
(merely a cluster of dwellings) turn left to pass Hamwood

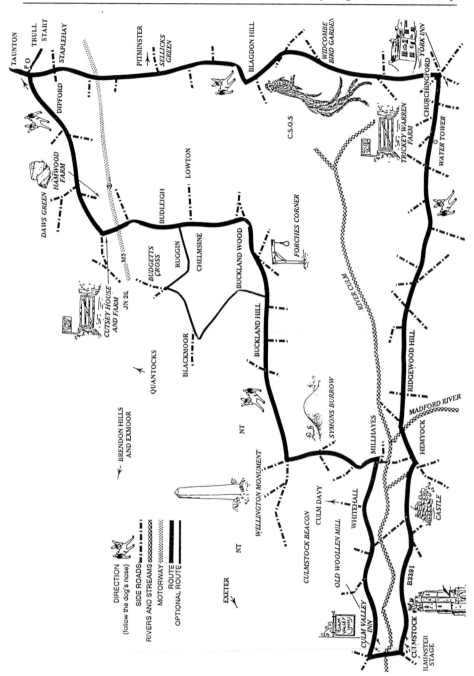

Farm where local cheese may be bought. The climb is followed by a short steep descent and a further rise to a junction (signposted Chelmsine), at which you turn left to cross the M5 after passing Cutsey House and Farm.

A series of "steps" now takes you up onto the northern slopes of the Blackdowns. With the tumult of traffic left behind the road bends sharply to the right to bring you up into Budleigh. At the next junction you have a choice:

◎ **Option 1.** At Forches Corner crossroads turn right for a gentle ascent over Buckland Hill, then the unusually pleasant feeling of a descent.

◎ Go straight on, ignoring two left turns, until you reach a T-junction at which you turn right to bring you to the ridge road at Forches Corner.

The Merry Harrier's hospitality is not to be enjoyed at present as this old coaching house stands closed and desolate. Once a gallows stood on this junction and local tales abound of ghosts and the appearance of the devil in the locality. The ridge road forms the Somerset/Devon border from Forches Corner until just beyond Wellington Hill on which stands Wellington Monument now owned by the National Trust.

**OR**

◎ **Option 2.** Instead of proceeding straight on you can turn right to enjoy a relatively level road through Ruggin to Budgett's Cross. Taking this option will give you an early view over the Vale of Taunton Deane to the Quantocks BUT you cannot escape forever. At Budgett's Cross turn left for the day's most challenging ascent. After three-quarters of a mile of steady ascent turn left at Blackmoor to climb Buckland Hill. Soon the roadside banks may be sufficiently colourfully clad with wild flowers to divert your attention from the labour of pedalling.

Where the road bends to the right the contours level off and you meet the ridge road just over half a mile from Forches Corner. Turn right to enjoy a slight descent.

◎ **(End of Option 2)**

◎ Go straight through two crossroads (you will pass a National Trust car park and view point between them on your right). About 200 yards beyond the second crossroads turn right into the car park that serves Wellington Monument.

A footpath leads to the "lofty column". Wheel your bike along the path (it is illegal to cycle along a footpath) through mixed woodland to the Monument. Constructed in honour of Sir Arthur Wellesley, Duke of Wellington, the obelisk enjoyed an enthusiastic start but was long in the completion. Although they had no direct connection with the town, the Duke's family had been connected with Somerset for centuries. For reasons that are not altogether clear Sir Arthur chose Wellington for his title. The citizens of the town, conscious of the honour, felt they ought to erect some permanent local memorial to him and chose a location at one of the highest points on the Blackdowns, 900 feet above sea level. The foundation stone was laid on 20th October 1817 in front of some 10,000 people with great ceremony. Soon afterwards, however, momentum was lost and the monument wasn't completed until the 1850s.

It was intended that the canons at the foot of the 175ft column should be those from the Battle of Waterloo. The existing canons are not; the Waterloo guns only got as far as Exeter Quay.

◎ After taking in a panorama of Quantock and Brendon Combes and the lush dairy lands of Taunton Vale return along the path to the ridge road. Turn left and, at the crossroads, right to "step" into Devon and Simonsburrow, a hamlet taking its name from the reputed burial chamber of Simon, the overlord of Exmoor who led the Blackdown tribes at the turn of the 8th century.

◎ The scenery takes on a softer mantle as you descend Combe Hill towards the River Culm and Hemyock. This is a "wide" road but care is still required as the lower part of the hill merits an "arrow" on the O.S. map. Also you have a right turn to make before reaching the river. The few houses that abut the road in the vicinity of this junction form Millhayes.

Millhayes was important as a staging post in the old coaching days and, upon the building of the Culm Valley Railway, was the station for Hemyock for the journey through to Tiverton Junction.

The right turn brings an unexpected but short-lived ascent before levelling out to follow the Culm through Whitehall to Culmstock. Go past the old woollen Mill and turn left to cross the Culm although you may wish firstly to partake of liquid refreshment in the pleasantly located Culm Valley Inn, the sign for which represents the old light railway. The Ilminster Stage is the other hostelry in the village and is found opposite All Saints Church.

The church is built of flint rubble masonry and boasts a yew tree growing out of the tower and a pre-reformation embroidery. The yew tree probably took root when the spire was taken down and is thought to be about 200 years old. R.D. Blackmore knew it as a boy in the 1830s when it was a well established tree. Culmstock is Perlycross in the author's novel of the same name. The embroidery is a 500 year old cope in gold depicting saints, apostles and martyrs together with the Blessed Virgin Mary and Christ.

◎ Whether you have quenched your thirst in the Culm Valley Inn or the Ilminster Stage you now proceed eastwards along the B3391 to Hemyock, the birthplace of The Young Farmers then called the Calf Club.

Look north towards Culmstock Beacon on Blackdown Common, one of the largest stretches of common land left on the hills. Wellington Monument is also visible on the skyline As you come into the village (Hamock at Domesday) the fragments of a feudal castle is on the right, separated from the church by a stream. Visit the interpretation

**All Saints Church, Culmstock**

Centre for an exposition of life at the castle from Medieval times through the ages to the 20th century. The castle is open from Easter to the end of September on Sundays and Bank Holidays and on Tuesdays and Thursdays in July and August from 2pm until 5pm.

◎ Follow the road round to the right then to the left when a memorial pump comes into view.

This commemorates the "glorious reign of Victoria, the Coronation of Edward VII and the restoration of peace in South Africa 1902".

◎ Ignore the turn "behind" the pump and take the next right turn (the "main" road swings round the left) to cross the River Madder after about half a mile. The road bends round to the right and climbs Ridgewood Hill towards Churchinford. Climb steadily (Hemyock is "protected" by hills to the north, south, east and west) for three-quarters of a mile. The lane then levels off. Enjoy a plateau for several miles ignoring turns to left and right. The York Inn at Churchinford is your short term destination. Shortly after a water tower appears on the right you come to a crossroads which you cross to descend to a village of Saxon origin that until recently benefited from its own bakery. You are welcomed by an inn dating from the 15th-16th century offering an excellent menu and ale to match. (A Cromwellian sword was found in a priest's chamber discovered during roof repairs.)

◎ Take the Blagdon road out of the village soon to pass Trickey Warren Farm and the multiple masts of the Composite Signals Observation Station. Continue past Widcombe Bird Gardens and straight ahead at the crossroads for a glorious descent of Blagdon ("wolf") Hill with further expansive views. This is another good road but beware the hairpin bend.

◎ The road brings you down through the village that bears the same name as the hill, then Staplehay, over the M5 and to

Trull. If you began your journey in Taunton cycle straight on into the town.

Folklore has it that fairies met regularly on the side of the Blackdowns near Pitminster holding a summer fair which human kind should not intrude upon. Back at Trull take time to admire the woodcraft of the bench ends in the church which date from the 16th century.

# West Somerset

# Ride 7

## Spiritual Sustenance & the Perfect Pub

**Route:**     Washford Station to Dunster.

**Distance:**  16 miles.

**Map:**       O.S. Landranger 1:50,000 Series Sheet 181.

---

◎ Catch the West Somerset Railway from any station to Washford.

◎ Turn left from the station and brave the A39 for less than a quarter of a mile before taking the first right turn signposted to Cleeve Abbey and Roadwater.

The Abbey, built from local red and yellow sandstone, was founded for Cistercian monks towards the end of the 12th century. Features to look for include the medieval tiled floor of the original dining hall, a magnificent 15th century timber roof carved with angels and a wall painting in the painted chamber. As you enter the precincts of the Abbey the gate-house welcomes you with the inscription, "Gate be open, shut to no honest person".

◎ Having sought spiritual sustenance turn left from the Abbey and very shortly fork right by the White Horse. The Washford River now runs on your left. A serious supping stop at the White Horse is probably best resisted so early along the route.

However, this stone hostelry has an interesting history; by 1730 it was a posting inn (the stables are still there) and was a toll-house, collecting funds for the local turnpike trust from 1765 to 1877.

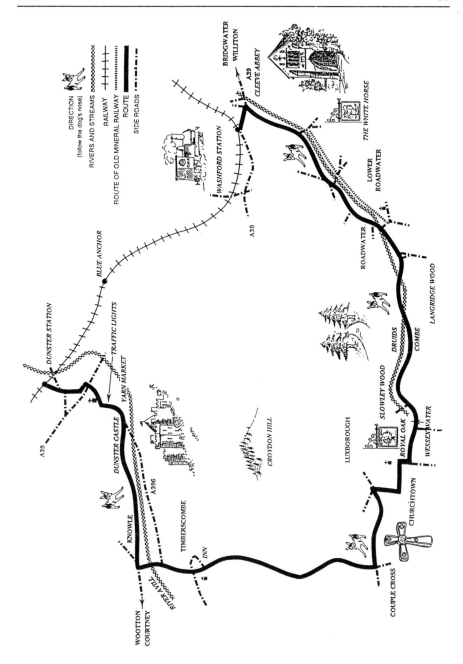

DIRECTION
(follow the dog's nose)

RIVERS AND STREAMS

RAILWAY

ROUTE OF OLD MINERAL RAILWAY

ROUTE

SIDE ROADS

BRIDGWATER

WILLITON

A39

CLEEVE ABBEY

THE WHITE HORSE

LOWER
ROADWATER

WASHFORD STATION

A39

ROADWATER

LANGRIDGE WOOD

BLUE ANCHOR

DUNSTER STATION

TRAFFIC LIGHTS

DRUIDS

COMBE

YARN MARKET

SLOWLEY WOOD

DUNSTER CASTLE

A39

CROYDON HILL

LUXBOROUGH

ROYAL OAK

WESSEX WATER

A396

KNOWLE

TIMBERSCOMBE

INN

CHURCHTOWN

COUPLE CROSS

RIVER AVILL

WOOTTON
COURTNEY

This route also follows the former West Somerset Mineral Railway which ran adjacent to the Washford River between Watchet and the iron ore mines in the Brendon Hills in the latter half of the nineteenth century and the first decade of this century. Part of the old railway line is now the subject of The West Somerset Mineral Railways Trail. Evidence of the line can be seen running alongside the river (see map).

◉ The road follows the Washford River up to Roadwater and the delightful Druid's Combe passing through Langridge and Slowley Woods and scenery to take your mind off a gentle but steady climb.

◉ The forest is mostly coniferous and owned by the Forestry Commission. Follow the road into Luxborough past handsome cottages and take the right turn over the hump-backed bridge to the Royal Oak.

Now your effort is well rewarded with a public house that is sheer perfection. A combination of excellent ales and food, inglenook with

**The Royal Oak, Luxborough**

log burning fire, flagstone floor, low-beamed ceilings make the formerly-named "Blazing Stump" a Somerset gem.

**Dying by Chocolate at The Royal Oak**

If you can drag yourself away further exquisite scenery awaits. (If the worst comes to the worst, you can always retrace your steps to Washford!)

◎ If you are seriously fit then you will not be daunted by the gradient that greets you when you remount. If, however, you are like me and fail to summon the self-discipline to dine lightly and walking doesn't injure your pride push the bike for the next quarter of a mile or so then consider remounting! You should have remounted by the church at Churchtown having swung to the right round a sharp bend where a road comes in from the left.

Set on the southern slopes of Croydon Hill Luxborough's parish church enjoys almost unrivalled tranquillity for these parts. The remains of what may be a Saxon cross are to be found in the churchyard to the south. A place of worship has existed on the site since the 12th century.

◎ At the next junction turn left. Follow this lane to Couple Cross (the name on the gate of the white house) where on a fine day far reaching views are enjoyed, particularly looking back towards the east where the valleys of the Brendons reveal themselves. Turn right for a delicious descent to Timberscombe. Beware of slippery, wet conditions; this is an uninterrupted descent partly through woodland. (Not far from Couple Cross, over to the right, the Welsh coast can be seen across the Bristol Channel). As you descend steeply past the church the road bends round to the right and past The Lion Hotel on your left. At the junction turn right then right again to pick up the A396 for no more than one third of a mile. At the next junction turn left to cross the Avill (signposted "Wootton Courtenay"). Another right turn brings you along a lane at the foot of Knowle and Grabbist Hills with the Avill valley on your right.

◎ This lane meets the A396 onto which you turn left to take you into the mainly medieval village of Dunster, overlooked by the fairytale Dunster Castle. Find time to seek out the Dovecote with a revolving ladder in the Old Rectory grounds and Dunster Water Mill (where stone-ground flour is still produced).

Numerous tea shops are scattered about the village.

◎ Cycle through the village up to the Yarn Market then past the Exmoor National Park Visitor Centre on your right to reach the A39. Cross using the underpass and when you emerge on the other side continue in the direction of Minehead. Take the second turn on the right (the first is signed, "No Entry") to reach Dunster Station.

**Dunster Castle from the Yarn Market**

# Ride 8

## *Hills, Steam and Sea*

**Route:**      Crowcombe Heathfield to Watchet
**Distance:**   14 miles
**Map:**        O.S. Landranger 1:50,000 Series Sheet 181, Minehead &
                Brendon Hills area

---

This trip creeps up on the Quantocks to afford expansive views of
The Brendon Hills and beyond.

**Advertisement at Crowcombe
Heathfield Station**

◎ Start from Crow-
combe Heathfield
Station with the time-
table in mind (trains
from Watchet run at
roughly two-hourly in-
tervals until 1700 –
1800 hours, depend-
ing on the season).
The trip takes about
two and a half hours
depending on length
of stay in tea rooms
and watering holes!

◎ Turn right from the
station to cycle along
the lane to a T-junc-
tion at which you turn

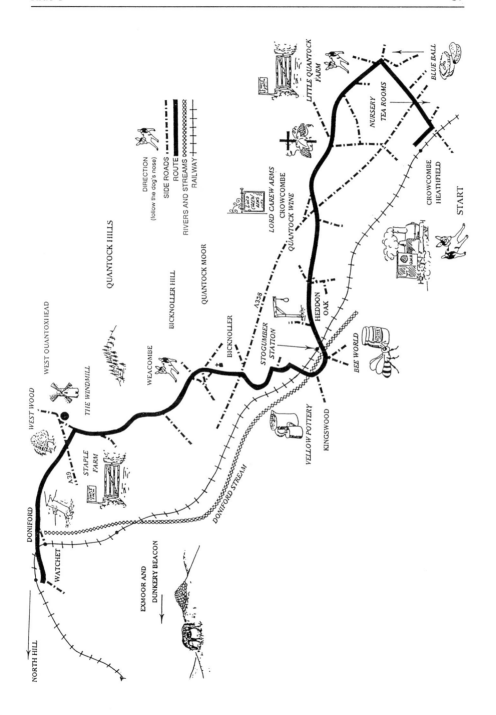

left. This tree lined avenue rises slightly to meet the A358. Turn left and almost immediately right WITH CARE for a gentle rise past the turning to Triscombe Nursery and then past a cream tea opportunity (to be saved until later on?) at Stable Cottage Restaurant &Tea Rooms. This road brings you into the hamlet of Triscombe. The main route takes you over the stream and sharply round to the left.

If, however, you turn right you'll come across the Blue Ball which, amongst other inviting fayre, offers pancakes ... huge pancakes! ... and good ale. In times gone by this hostelry held a whortle-pie rival (Revel) at the end of the whortleberry picking season. At the "Rival" whortleberry pie was consumed with ale.

◉ Returning to the intended route you may wish to push the bike up a short steep slope of 50 yards or so, especially if you have "over-faced" yourself. The agony is short-lived. Soon you are "contouring" the slopes of Great Hill shortly to pass Little Quantock Farm on your right as the lane turns sharply left. Ignore the next left turn and head down taking EXTREME CARE as the gradient merits an "arrow" on the O.S. map. You may even choose to dismount, especially if the conditions are wet and slippery. At the junction bear left and turn right at the next to enter the village of Crowcombe.

You will see the Church of the Holy Ghost on the right and, opposite, the Church House. The latter was a social centre for local people and hosted assemblies gathering for e.g. festivals celebrating the dedication of the church at which there were fun and games with eating and drinking. Its current use includes art exhibitions.

The church should be visited for an inspection of the south aisle and the pre-Reformation pews. The excellent carvings in the bench ends depict, amongst other themes, vines as a symbol of fecundity.

◉ Back in the saddle, pass the Market Cross (dating from 1226) on the right and the Lord Carew Arms on the left unless you feel drawn to partake of its hospitality.

The Carews are descendants of the original owners of Crowcombe Court and the north aisle of the church is a private family chapel.

◎ Continue up through the village and, just past Quantock Wine Shippers, turn left to meet and cross the A358. A pleasant descent gives you the momentum to overcome the lower part of the hill that climbs towards Heddon Oak (the site of gallows in times of old). Don't forget to change gear!

A gateway on your right towards the brow of the hill rewards you with glorious views over Thorncombe and Bicknoller Hills and Quantock Moor.

◎ After an "up", a "down" takes you past Quarkhill Fruit Farm. Go past the turning to Culverhayes and cycle under the railway bridge.

Immediately on the left is Bee World where the legs can be stretched along the nature trail and tea supped in an idyllic setting.

◎ Return to the road and take the next right to follow the Doniford Stream through Kingswood. You now cycle up and down a succession of short steep slopes then come to a junction. The road dips severely so EXERCISE CAUTION as you turn right (bum back in saddle and controlled pressure on the REAR brake).

◎ The lane bends to the left then right before rising under another railway bridge and turning left again.

The banks on the sides of these lanes are sumptuously clad with a succession of wild flowers from early March onwards. Expect to see primroses, dog's mercury, delicate dog violets and stitchwort around mid-March.

◎ At the next junction turn left. The lane may be slippery if wet – these are farm lanes after all. A further 90 degree bend brings you to the A358 yet again. Turn left and then right to climb gently to Bicknoller at the foot of the hill of the same

name already seen from the west side of the Doniford Valley.
Yet another hostelry awaits.

The church has its attendant yew tree and the weather cock shows
evidence of use as target practice.

◎ Cycle up Church Lane then left along Trendle and Honeyrow
Lanes. At the end of Honeyrow Lane turn right for a climb up
past Weacombe to West Quantoxhead. Just past Staple
Farm turn left to descend to the A39. Cross over with care to
continue your descent towards Doniford with West Wood on
your right. Not only are you hit with a glorious coastal vista
but, to the west, North Hill rises beyond Minehead. The
Brendon and Exmoor Hills add to this exquisite scenery.

◎ Your descent is almost unbroken for a mile. The road is good
but beware holiday traffic. Pass Doniford Halt (you will pass
through it courtesy of steam or diesel train shortly). Continue
through a residential area until the road bends sharply to the
left and, there before you, is Watchet Station.

If you have time, you should explore the town with its ancient
harbour. The town's ancient name is said to have been Veched
possibly from an older name for the Washford River. Part of the
harbour was constructed by Sir W. Wyndham, Queen Anne's Secretary of State for War. Following the closing down of the iron ore
mines merchandise passing through the port was limited to flour,
timber and paper at the tail end of the eighteenth century.

# Ride 9

## Encounter with a Green Man

**Route:** Crowcombe Heathfield to Stogumber
**Distance:** 16 miles
**Map:** O.S. Landranger 1:50,000 Series; Sheet 181, Minehead & Brendon Hills

---

◎ This route follows a large part of Hills, Steam and Sea (ROUTE 8). Follow the directions for that route to West Quantoxhead but do NOT turn left past Staple Farm.

Highland cattle once roamed the Quantocks in this vicinity and hereabouts an ancient trackway, "The Great Road" runs out.

◎ Thirsty? Go up over the brow of the hill to descend to the A39. Immediately, on the right, is the Windmill Inn, a free house offering good food, a beer garden and extensive coastal views from its lounge bar.

◎ After quenching the thirst return through the village to the fork where the road you came up bends round to the left. Fork right and head down to the A358.

◎ Go straight across and straight on over the West Somerset Railway and Doniford Stream before turning left along the level (yes, really!) for a few hundred yards towards Vellow.

The pottery is well worth a visit.

◎ The road bends sharply right then left and climbs into Stogumber.

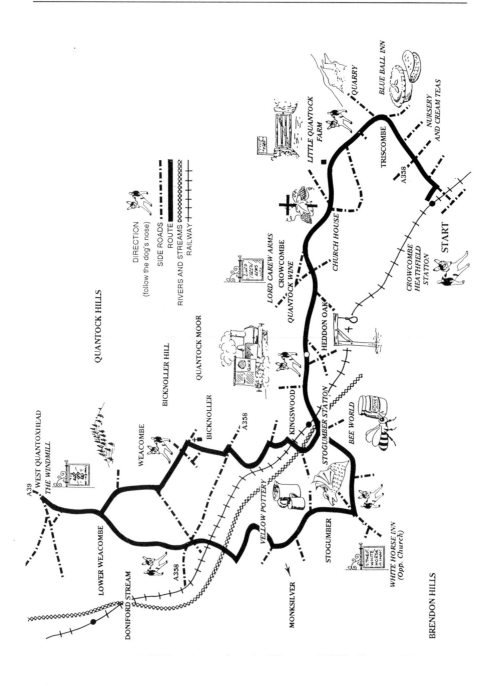

Geographically in the Brendon foothills, the parish of Stogumber extends into the Quantocks. However, red sandstone gives way to white, grey and cream buildings in this delightful village blissfully free from uniformity of architectural style.

◎ Turn left to take in the White Horse Inn which has added to itself the 18th century reading room, the door of which is placed at the top of a curved flight of steps.

Across the way from the pub is the Church of Our Lady St. Mary. Look for the Green Man, a primitive fertility symbol evidently tolerated in local churches.

◎ Take the road out of the village that is signposted Crowcombe Heathfield and head for Stogumber Station but not without first visiting the Wildlife Centre at Bee World. If time permits explore the Nature Trail or have the cup of tea you didn't have time for when passing the Centre earlier in the day.

◎ The station is only a stone's throw away.

**Winsford Hill, Exmoor**

# Exmoor

# Ride 10

## *Bronze Age Barrows & Celtic Cenotaph*

**Route:**      Exford – Winsford – Withypool – Exford

**Distance:**   20 miles

**Map:**        O.S. Landranger 1:50,000 Series; Sheet 181, Minehead
                & The Brendon Hills

---

This round trip is best undertaken out of the "season". I first cycled
it on a crisp, clear October day when the trees were changing colour
and the gorse and heather gave a vibrant cladding to the moors,
commons and "allotments". Level pedalling comes as a luxury.

◉ Begin in the public car park in Exford (Grid Reference
854384; O.S. Landranger 1:50,000 Series Sheet 181, Minehead & The Brendon Hills) the lane to which is almost
opposite the Crown Hotel.

Exford is very much the geographical centre of Exmoor National
Park so it is hardly surprising that it is the focal point for tourists.
The village's history is inextricably linked with hunting which has
been the source of employment for large numbers over the centuries
(a reported fact not a commendation).

Of the public houses and hotels, the White Horse Inn seems to attract
most "trippers" while the Crown is a quieter locals' hostelry. I can
vouch for the quality of the food at the latter and have good reports
of the former. Not to be forgotten is the Exmoor House Hotel.
However, lingering for other than a tea or coffee might induce inertia
so ...

◉ Cycle up to the B3224 and turn right to be faced by a not
insignificant incline which merits one arrow on the O.S. Map.

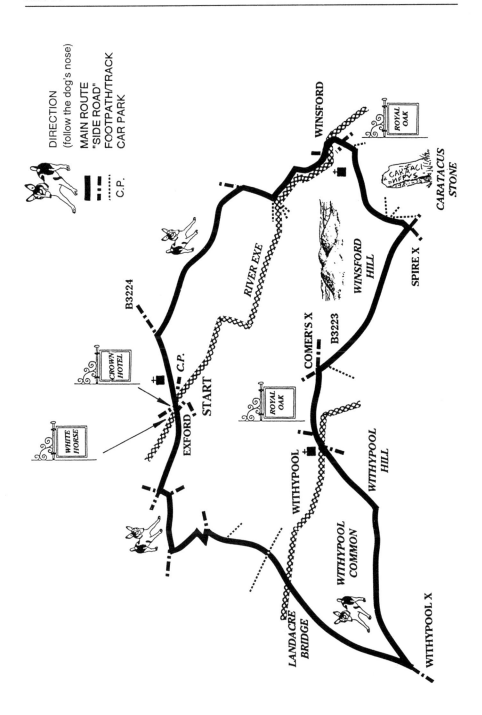

It is short lived; the road levels out as you reach St. Salvyn's Church, situated close to the route of a prehistoric trackway. About half a mile from the church take the right turn to Winsford and enjoy the first sustained descent of the day, for four miles.

◎ Where the road bends sharply to the right and along the foot of the spruce clad Staddon Hill see if you can determine the site of an Iron Age Fort. Continue to follow the Larcombe Brooke and then the Exe into which the Larcombe flows at Kemps. You will soon find yourself in the village of Winsford, birthplace of Ernest Bevin, trade union leader and former Foreign Secretary.

The slate roofed grey cottage opposite the Post Office/Shop is where this great statesman was born.

◎ You need the Hawkridge road out of the village which takes you past the Green on your right and the old thatched Royal Oak for which I was too early, but it gave every appearance

**The Royal Oak, Winsford**

of living up to its name (see the references to other "Royal Oaks" in the preceding route descriptions).

In his book, "An Exploration of Exmoor and the Hill Country of West Somerset" John Ll. W. Page (a member of the Somersetshire Archeological and Natural History Society) describes the pub in the following terms. "There is a wonderfully picturesque inn, the Royal Oak, with mossy thatch and projecting windows ..." He was writing at the end of the last century and little has changed. Page was quite enchanted by the whole village and continues his description of, "divers quaint cottages, and a curious old paved bridge, covered with ferns, spanning the Exe, one of six – not all over the Exe – for Winsford has nearly as many as London, though most are of Lilliputian proportions."

◉ The lane you are cycling along is Halse Lane and it climbs, quite steeply at first, up past Townsend Cottages and Halse Farm.

The gateways in the hedgerows on the right give fine views over the valley of the Winn Brook.

◉ Approximately one mile from Winsford you cycle over the first of countless cattle grids to continue along an unfenced road with the lower slopes of Winsford Hill on the right and "The Allotment" on the left. The reason for choosing this route out of Winsford, in preference to the marginally gentler Ash Lane soon becomes apparent for about two hundred yards on the nearside of the crossroads which you are approaching is the "Caratacus Stone".

This Celtic monument bears the Latin inscription, "Carataci nepus" – "clansmen of Caratacus" and dates back to 500 AD. It is leased to the National Trust for 500 years from 1918. Page assumed the stone to be one of those standing stones often found in Cornwall and Devon and believed it to be the only specimen of its kind in Somerset.

◉ To reach the monument you need to dismount at a junction

of three footpaths and take the path nearest to the road. This leads to the monument which now enjoys the protection of a shelter. To return to the route retrace your steps to the point where you left the lane and continue up to the crossroads, Spire Cross. Turn right to climb steadily to the summit of Winsford Hill.

When visibility is good the views are outstanding. From the Trig. Point, a short distance from the road, you can see as far as Exmoor's highest point, Dunkery Beacon to the north. It is worth wheeling the bike to the Trig. Point just for a closer acquaintance with the closest of the three "Wambarrows". These are a group of burial mounds of Bronze Age chiefs.

◎ Continue down the north west side of Winsford Hill and, at the crossroads (Comers Cross), prepare for a steep descent to Withypool and the Royal Oak which meets one's expectations. R.D. Blackmore was an occasional visitor here. Refreshed and replete return to the saddle to continue an exploration of one of Exmoor's oldest settlements.

Withypool takes its name from a river running in a valley of ash trees. Surrounded by common and moorland, the village was relatively isolated in past centuries due to poor tracks and roads across some treacherously boggy terrain.

◎ After crossing the River Barle take the right turn that temporarily relieves you from pedalling steeply up hill. Close wooded valleys are left behind as a wilder more rugged landscape emerges. The road climbs steadily before levelling off near the ancient trackway that leads off to the left. As you approach the hairpin bend at Portford Bridge harder pedalling is required.

Evidence of settlement by prehistoric man abounds in the form of a stone circle and tumulus on top of Withypool Hill to your left and, as a reward for the effort of that pull up from the bridge, Brightworthy Barrows to your right.

◎ As you pass Hawkridge Common on top of which sit Brightworthy Barrows enjoy the rare sensation of pedalling on the level. Three-quarters of a mile after the next cattle grid turn right (Exford 4¾ miles) for an exhilarating descent to the 15th century Landacre Bridge. Alas the descent is balanced by a sustained steep ascent after a deceptively gentle start. The agony isn't too prolonged. As you traverse the route of The Two Moors Way and cycle along an unfenced road the going gets much easier.

◎ About 300 yards after the next cattle grid turn left for the route to Exford signed "avoiding ford ". Beware the hairpin bend as you drop to the Pennycombe Water. Climb to a T-junction passing overgrown quarries on your right. Turn right to contour for about a mile to the junction with the B3223. Turn left shortly to meet the B3224 at White Cross. Sail down this road to cross the Exe and reward yourself at one of the previously mentioned watering holes!

# Ride 11

## *Industrial Heartland*

**Route:**     Wimbleball Lake – Luxborough – Roadwater –
Treborough – Wimbleball Lake

**Distance:** 20 miles

**Map:**       Landranger 1:50,000 Series; Sheet 181, Minehead & the
Brendon Hills

---

This route bestows majestic views of Wimbleball Lake with Haddon
Hill beyond, Croydon's forested slopes and the tumbling combes of
the Brendons' northern flanks. Again level pedalling is not a regular
feature of the day but sustained free-wheeling, enchanting scenery
and the Royal Oak at Luxborough reward hard pedalling. Evidence
of Exmoor's industrial heritage is secreted among the wooded folds
between the romantically titled "Druid's Combe" and the Brendon
Ridge.

◎ Begin in the Wessex Water Car Park at the northern end of
Wimbleball Lake (Grid Reference 974319). Toilets are available here.

Take a few minutes to scan the reservoir and its surroundings.
Herons make a regular appearance and kestrels hover over the
occasional copse. The lake was constructed by damming the River
Haddeo in the 1970s in response to the late twentieth century's
demand for recreational and leisure facilities.

◎ From the car park turn left and, at the T-junction, left again to
descend gently over the "neck" of the lake. Rise to a T-junction at which you turn right (signposted to Blagdon Ford) for

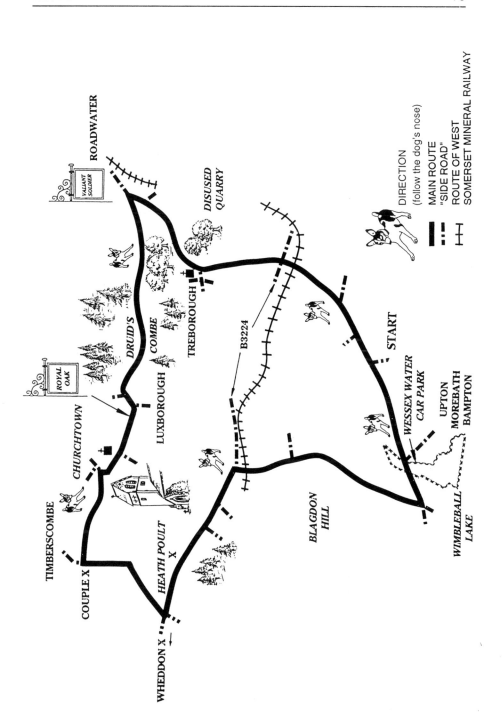

DIRECTION
(follow the dog's nose)
MAIN ROUTE
"SIDE ROAD"
ROUTE OF WEST
SOMERSET MINERAL RAILWAY

a climb to the summit of Blagdon Hill. Continue down to Blagdon Farm after which there is an unexpected pull to bring you to the B3224. (In wet weather this road can be slippery.) Turn left for a relatively level couple of miles to the crossroads at Heath Poult Cross.

◎ Turn right in the direction of Timberscombe and Luxborough. With the exception of a couple of "blips" you are about to embark on a glorious sustained descent of some four miles. Momentum should secure that the aberrations cause few problems. Drop down from Lype Hill to the T-junction at Couple Cross (the name on the gate of the white house) and turn right. Follow this lane, enjoying extensive views over Croydon and Monksham Hills to the north and the green amphitheatre of the valley that carries a stream from Chargot Wood to the house of the same name, to a junction. Turn right to descend to Churchtown, the upper end of the strung out village of Luxborough.

St. Mary's, a Grade II Listed Building, enjoys an idyllic and tranquil setting. The lower part of its unusual saddleback tower dates from the 14th century; the chancel from a century earlier.

◎ The final part of your descent to the Royal Oak is particularly steep (20%) and winding. BEWARE. See the route, "Washford To Dunster" for a description of this rather special hostelry.

◎ When you can no longer justify lingering in the "Blazing Stump" climb back into the saddle, cross the bridge and turn left for a relaxed top gear descent through Druid's Combe which carries a tributary of the Washford River.

Whether there is a valid association with Druidism is open to debate; an older name is Drucombe.

◎ The lane through the combe crosses the stream twice. As

you cross the second time you cycle through Langridge Wood (taking its name from a long ridge).

In 1820, workmen, clearing the hillside to make a road for hauling timber, came across a stone chest (kist/kistaven) which contained a man's skeleton. Buried in a pre-Christian era, his reinternment in Treborough's churchyard seems somewhat anomalous.

◉ Continue down towards Roadwater and turn left at the next junction soon to pass The Valiant Soldier on your left.

The real purpose of a visit to this linear village is to seek out evidence of the old West Somerset Mineral Railway. If you cycle to the telephone box and turn right down the lane the line of the old railway line is evident on the east side of the river.

The line, which ran from the old port of Watchet to the top of Brendon Hill via Roadwater and Comberow, was built in 1857. From Comberow to the top of Brendon Hill a gradient of 1:4 for three-quarters of a mile had to be overcome. The freight was iron ore from mines near Ralegh's Cross which was shipped from Watchet to Wales by the Ebbw Vale Company. Mining ceased in 1883 possibly due to the influx of iron ore from Spain and the high costs of transport from Watchet to Wales. A passenger service to Comberow survived until 1898. Passengers were transferred from the train to a comfortably fitted truck and drawn by fixed engine to the summit.

◉ To continue the route turn round and cycle back past the Valiant Soldier to the fork where the signpost points towards Treborough. Continue towards Treborough; a sustained climb begins. Although the going is steep for the next two to three miles motorised traffic is rare and you pass through Treborough Woods and the disused slate quarries, now a Conservation Area.

Superb views are guaranteed and there is some respite if you visit the tiny settlement of Treborough and its parish church.

◉ To reach Treborough turn "right" at the next junction instead of following the road round to the left. The church is reached from the next lane on your right.

As a piece of architecture the church is disappointing but you will find in the guide reference to the reinternment of "Treborough Man" and to the location of his previous burial spot, 120 yards NNE of the church.

◎ Return to the saddle and to the junction where you took a "right" turn for the village. Turn right for a slightly less demanding climb to meet the B3224 at Sminhays Corner.

About 80 yards from the top, on your right, is Sminhays Cottage, an isolated but idyllic dwelling.

◎ At the T-junction turn right onto the B road then immediately left to cross the old railway once again. Descend to the next junction and turn right. After a brief and relatively gentle undulation settle into an exhilarating mile downhill towards Wimbleball Lake. Don't forget to turn left before you cross the bridge to return to the car park.

# DEVON:
## East Devon

# Ride 12

## *Whiteways, Wool, and Wilts United*

**Route:**     Whimple or Broadhembury to Uffculme, and back
**Distance:**  35 miles or 20 miles
**Map:**       O.S. Landranger 1:50,000 Series; Sheets 181 and 192.

---

◎ This route can be started from either The Square in Whimple
   or the centre of Broadhembury. This description begins in
   Whimple.

If you know of the village of Whimple it is likely to be because of its
association with Whiteways' Orchards. In 1894 Henry Whiteway,
using a former tanyard, began the cider firm that became famous
across the world. Apples were transported by rail to Whimple
Station which is adjacent to the site of the old factory at Slewton.
The Tom Putt was a favoured type of cider apple. By 1900 markets
had been established as far afield as India, Australia and South
Africa. The business boomed well into the second half of this
century but mergers in the Sixties led to decline and closure.

◎ From the Square, turn left taking care due to the blind bend
   past the thatched post office. Follow the road under the
   railway bridge and round to the right past the Thirsty Farmer
   public house. Climb gradually and take the first left turn to
   Talaton. An undulating route takes you into a village that
   boasts an excellent shop owned as a co-operative by the
   residents.

◎ Take the road opposite the Talaton Inn for a short climb to
   Bittery Cross, the site of gibbets from which were hung

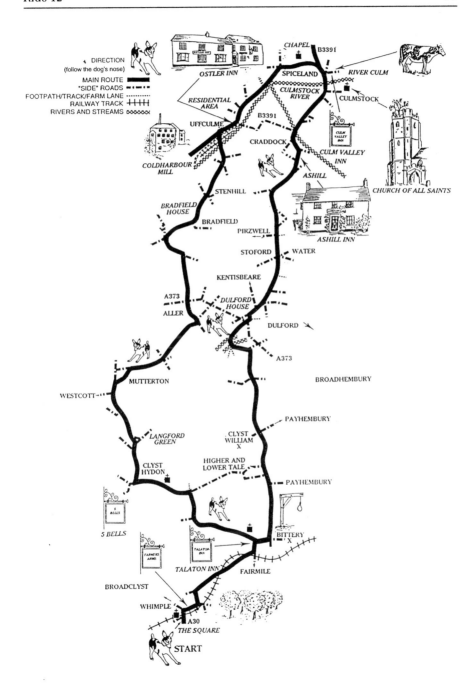

DIRECTION
(follow the dog's nose)
MAIN ROUTE
"SIDE" ROADS
FOOTPATH/TRACK/FARM LANE
RAILWAY TRACK
RIVERS AND STREAMS

CHAPEL B3391
SPICELAND
RIVER CULM
OSTLER INN
CULMSTOCK RIVER
CULMSTOCK
RESIDENTIAL AREA
UFFCULME
B3391
CRADDOCK
CULM VALLEY INN
COLDHARBOUR MILL
ASHILL
STENHILL
CHURCH OF ALL SAINTS
BRADFIELD HOUSE
BRADFIELD
PIRZWELL
ASHILL INN
STOFORD WATER
KENTISBEARE
A373
DULFORD HOUSE
ALLER
DULFORD
A373
MUTTERTON
BROADHEMBURY
WESTCOTT
PAYHEMBURY
LANGFORD GREEN
CLYST WILLIAM X
CLYST HYDON
HIGHER AND LOWER TALE
PAYHEMBURY
5 BELLS
BITTERY X
FARMERS ARMS
TALATON INN
TALATON INN
FAIRMILE
BROADCLYST
WHIMPLE
A30
THE SQUARE
START

supporters of James, Duke of Monmouth. Turn left for a delightful gently undulating couple of miles to Clyst William Cross.

From March onwards the banks and hedgerows are covered with wild flowers. Primroses are succeeded by stitchwort,dog violets, bluebells, campion, vetch, the occasional orchid and speedwell.

◎ From Clyst William Cross continue northwards with the southwest slopes of the Blackdown Hills visible to your right. About two miles on (after another crossroads) turn left to negotiate two small fords and follow the road to meet the A373 at Dulford. Cross over the main road. The lane you are now on dog-legs left to meet a T-junction at which you turn right opposite the gateway to Dulford House. Now take the second left turn to Stoford Water, little more than a five-lane crossroads. Go "straight on" towards Ashill over the stream. A steepish climb takes you past much larger fields than those seen earlier and past a turn to Pirzwell. This is a lane neither for fast traffic nor wide vehicles. Come the end of July there's a chance of encroachment by wayside vegetation.

◎ Up means down and before long you can enjoy a quiet descent to Ashill and, perhaps, liquid refreshment at the inn of the same name. Continue down to the junction, turn left and follow signs to Culmstock. You will cycle through Craddock to emerge onto the B3391 crossing a tributary of the Culm *en route*. The road drops down to the Culm but you take a right turn towards Hemyock as it bends to the left.

Almost immediately, you are confronted with the Church of All Saints with the yew tree growing from its tower. For more information on the church refer to the route description for "Rivers and Ruins", ride 14. Culmstock was the site of a depot for The Culm Valley Dairy Company, taken over by the Wilts United Dairy. The company's home was Hemyock (birthplace of the Young Farmers) and it was responsible for the now traditional once-a-day milk collection. Previously, the mixing of two milkings had been considered unsuitable. The coming of the Culm Valley railway greatly assisted the speed of milk collection and delivery.

◎ From the church return to the B3191 and cycle over the Culm past the Culm Valley Inn. The road swings round to the left and you climb for a short distance before taking a left turn to Prescott and Uffculme. You will soon pass Spicelands on the left where a Quaker Meeting House was built in 1670.

The Five Mile Act of 1665 barred any non-conformist preacher from returning to within five miles of where he had preached before the passing of the Act. A consequence was the establishment of Non-conformist meeting places in remote locations.

◎ At the next junction turn left to drop down to Five Fords before rising slightly. The lane runs quite close to the river before swinging away to bring you into the northern part of Uffculme.

Settled by the Saxons around the 8th century, the village takes its name from "Uffa's settlement on the Culm". It was of greater significance when there were a number of woollen and worsted mills, not to mention a brewery.

◎ Pass the Ostler Inn and take the left turn opposite the chapel to descend to Coldharbour Mill which is still in action and is open to the public.

It's worth stopping to take advantage of a guided tour and the small restaurant which serves its hot dogs with real sausages.

◎ From the Mill turn right to cross the old railway route and the Culm before a short lived climb to Stenhill and a descent to Bradfield. The road bends to the right and you pass the private chapel to Bradfield House before seeing the drive to the largely Jacobean and late Medieval structure which stands on the site of a 13th century house

You have now left behind the steeper gradients of the Blackdowns; a gentler rolling open terrain awaits you.

◎ Less than half a mile from Bradfield House a road from Willand joins from the right and you take a sharp turn to the left. At the next junction turn right. You will meet the A373. Go straight ahead to Aller then right at the crossroads to Mutterton. At the five-lane crossroads go straight ahead for about a mile. You come to a junction at which you turn left to Clyst Hydon. The signpost says Westcott. You pass the old 1893 Mutterton Dairy on your left. Follow this road over the River Weaver and through Langford Green. About a mile from Langford Green you come to a junction. A right turn will lead you towards a rather large but welcoming hostelry, the Five Bells. The principal route requires you to follow the 90 degree bend to the left to pass through the strung out village of Clyst Hydon, one of a number of villages which takes its name from the River Clyst which rises in the Blackdowns and flows to the River Exe at Topsham.

As you might imagine the pub takes its name from the five bells in the peal at St. Andrews church.

◎ At the "end" of the village the road bends sharply round to the right then, three-quarters of a mile further on, sharply to the left bringing you up towards Talaton. From here retrace your steps to Whimple.

**Broadhembury Option**

◎ Beginning at the Drewe Arms, go down through the village to cross the stream and turn left to cycle to the crossroads at Causeway End. Turn right to climb for a short distance before the gradient eases. At the next crossroads go straight on. At the next staggered junction turn left. You come to another crossroads. Turn right to find yourself on the lane to Stoford Water. You are now on the main route.

◎ To return to Broadhembury from Clyst Hydon, instead of following the 90 degree bend to the right at the "end" of the village take the "left" turn to Tale. Follow this lane to a T-junction at Higher Tale. Turn left. The lane bends sharply right through Lower Tale and comes to a T-junction. Turn left and at Clyst William Cross turn right, cycle down to Danes Mill and over the stream. The road bends round to the right to meet another T-junction. Turn left and at Colliton Cross go straight over the A373 and follow the lane into Broadhembury.

**The Drewe Arms, Broadhembury**

# Ride 13

## *A Satisfying Saunter Savouring Distant Slopes*

**Route:**     Whimple – Talaton – Kentisbeare Clyst Hydon – Whimple

**Distance:** Approximately 20 miles.

**Map:**       O.S. Landranger 1:50,000 Series; Sheet 192.

---

Refreshingly free from steep gradients but affords excellent views of the western flanks of the Blackdown Hills. A satisfying saunter savouring distant slopes.

◎ Start at Whimple (see Route "Whiteways, Wool and Wilts United").

◎ Cycle to Talaton then Clyst William Cross. Continue northwards over a crossroads until you arrive at a junction at which you turn left to St Andrews Wood. You will have cycled through a small copse shortly before reaching the junction. The wood is left behind as you cycle on the level soon to cross the first of two fords as the lane bends sharply to the right. The second ford follows quickly then you rise to meet the A373 at Dulford. Go straight ahead at the crossroads and when you reach a T-junction turn right. Take the second left towards Stoford Water and then the Ashill road northwards and slightly upwards. Note the much larger fields on the left; arable and dairy farming are practised in this area.

◎ Take the left turn to Pirzwell but BEWARE slippery mucky surfaces in wet weather. At the next junction turn left to

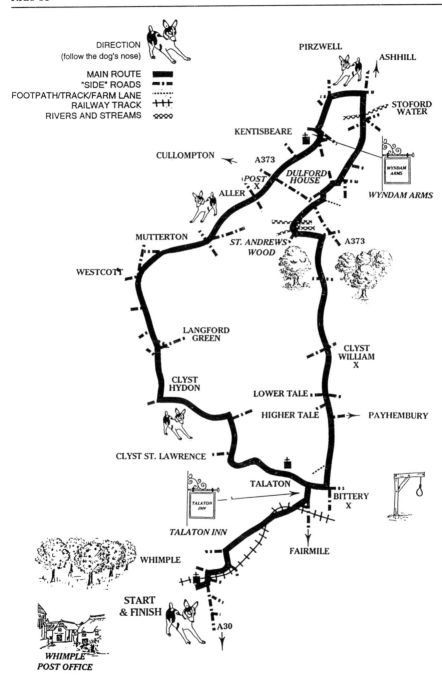

DIRECTION
(follow the dog's nose)

MAIN ROUTE
"SIDE" ROADS
FOOTPATH/TRACK/FARM LANE
RAILWAY TRACK
RIVERS AND STREAMS

PIRZWELL

ASHHILL

STOFORD
WATER

KENTISBEARE

CULLOMPTON

A373

DULFORD
HOUSE

*WYNDAM
ARMS*

POST
X

ALLER

*WYNDAM ARMS*

MUTTERTON

*ST. ANDREWS
WOOD*

A373

WESTCOTT

LANGFORD
GREEN

CLYST
WILLIAM
X

CLYST
HYDON

LOWER TALE

HIGHER TALE

PAYHEMBURY

CLYST ST. LAWRENCE

TALATON

BITTERY
X

*TALATON
INN*

*TALATON INN*

FAIRMILE

WHIMPLE

START
& FINISH

A30

*WHIMPLE
POST OFFICE*

descend to Kentisbeare, an attractive village aptly described as "the western gateway to the hills". Turn left opposite the Wyndham Arms public house (or not as the case may be!) then bear right and right again (signposted Cullompton) for a top gear pedal to meet the A373 at Post Cross. Go straight across shortly to come to another crossroads which you cross. At the next crossroads go straight on to Mutterton. This is hospitable cycling terrain; relish it! You are now on the return route for the "Whiteways, Wool and Wilts United" ride (ride 12). At the next junction turn left to Clyst Hydon (it's signposted "Westcott") then make your way back to Whimple via Talaton.

◉ (Refer to the directions for "Whiteways Wool & Wilts United" from "Follow this road over the River Weaver and through Langford Green.")

# Ride 14

## *Rivers and Ruins*

**Route:**    Whimple or Broadhembury to Hemyock, Dunkeswell Abbey and back

**Distance:**  20 miles or 35 miles

**Map:**     O.S. Landranger 1:50,000 Series; Sheets 181 and 192.

---

This ride starts either from the Square in Whimple or in Broadhembury village centre.

**From Whimple**

Associated with Whiteways Orchards, Whimple is a delightful Devon village with a small tributary of the River Clyst running through the middle past the church.

◎ From the Square, turn left taking care due to the blind bend past the thatched post office. Follow the road under the railway bridge and round to the right past The Thirsty Farmer public house. Climb gradually and take the first left turn to Talaton. An undulating route takes you into a village that boasts an excellent shop owned as a co-operative by the residents.

If sustenance is required at this early stage a sausage plait absolutely stuffed with meat will see you through the best part of the day. Alternatively snacks to meet a vegetarian diet can be obtained. Hidden from the main street is the 15th century church of St. James with a notable display of gargoyles.

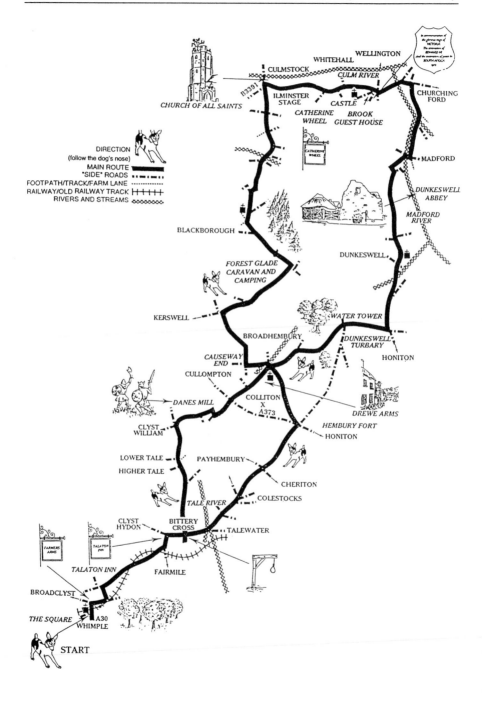

DIRECTION
(follow the dog's nose)
MAIN ROUTE
"SIDE" ROADS
FOOTPATH/TRACK/FARM LANE
RAILWAY/OLD RAILWAY TRACK
RIVERS AND STREAMS

WELLINGTON
WHITEHALL
CULMSTOCK
CULM RIVER
CHURCHING
FORD
ILMINSTER
STAGE
CASTLE
CHURCH OF ALL SAINTS
CATHERINE
WHEEL
BROOK
GUEST HOUSE
B3391

MADFORD
DUNKESWELL
ABBEY
MADFORD
RIVER
BLACKBOROUGH
FOREST GLADE
CARAVAN AND
CAMPING
DUNKESWELL
KERSWELL
WATER TOWER
BROADHEMBURY
DUNKESWELL
TURBARY
HONITON
CAUSEWAY
END
CULLOMPTON
DANES MILL
COLLITON
X
A373
DREWE ARMS
CLYST
WILLIAM
HEMBURY FORT
HONITON
LOWER TALE
HIGHER TALE
PAYHEMBURY
CHERITON
COLESTOCKS
TALE RIVER
CLYST
HYDON
BITTERY
CROSS
TALEWATER
FARMERS
ARMS
TALATON
INN
TALATON INN
FAIRMILE
BROADCLYST
THE SQUARE
A30
WHIMPLE
START

◉ Take the road opposite the Talaton Inn for a short climb to Bittery Cross, the site of gibbets from which were hung supporters of James, Duke of Monmouth.

These men had been working on the construction of a fine new house at Escot a few miles away. They downed tools to join the rebel army in June 1685 at Lyme Regis.

◉ Turn left for a delightful gently undulating couple of miles.

To the right the south west slopes of the Blackdown Hills, an Area of Outstanding Natural Beauty, stretch out.

◉ At Clyst William Cross take the right turn, signposted Payhembury, descending to Danes Mill and, half a mile on, turn left to bring you up to the A373 at Colliton Cross.

From Bittery Cross, in April and May,the hedges and banks are host to a profusion of purple and pink. Campions, speedwell, bluebells, herb robert, dog violets and orchids abound mingling with stitchwort, yellow archangel, dead-nettles and dog's mercury.

Note two rather fine 1927 dwellings on the left as you approach the main road, (home then to postman and policeman).

◉ Go over the A373 for another glorious lane that takes you into the Conservation village of Broadhembury.

Situated to the north of Hembury Fort, from which both this and the neighbouring village of Payhembury take their names, Broadhembury consists of thatched cob and stone dwellings constructed during the 14th and 15th centuries. It represents a typical nucleated Saxon village.

Ready for an early lunch? A wooden bench presents itself for an impromptu al fresco snack. In competition, the Drewe Arms, possibly the old church house offers an excellent selection of real ales, an extensive menu and comfortable characterful surroundings.

**From Broadhembury**

◉ Leave Broadhembury by the lane that crosses the stream at

the western end of the village and make for the crossroads at Causeway End. Prepare yourself mentally for the day's first real effort! Turn right and upwards, moderately, before the lane levels out past Upcott Farm. At the next crossroads turn right for a steeper climb to the edge of Knowle Wood where you turn right to encounter a 20% gradient. The author dismounts at this point. The exquisite scenery has to be properly appreciated and vehicular traffic combined with a sharp left hand bend are not conducive to either that appreciation or safety!

Mixed woodland and its accompanying wayside flora contrive to divert your attention from the effort of pushing or pedalling. In May it's easy to lose count of the number of wild flowers.

◎ Soon you're back on the level and cycling past Forest Glade Camping and Caravan Site. Turn left at the T-junction and enjoy a controlled descent into Blackborough, a seemingly strung out village that sits atop Saint Hill and Ponchydown and owes its existence to the whetstone mining industry. Manned mostly by the Cornish, trade lost out to Spanish competition.

The church of All Saints bears little comparison with Somerset's finest but this mid-19th century spired church commands an imposing situation and here begins a sustained descent of nearly two miles to a tributary of the River Culm.

◎ Following the Culmstock signs will give you expansive views of the western end of the Blackdowns as you cross the stream for a short lived climb.

◎ Soon you are descending again to meet the B3391 onto which you turn right before taking a right turn on a tight bend in the direction of Hemyock.

You are faced with the flint built church of All Saints and its tower, host for some centuries to a yew tree. This church is worthy of a visit not least to view the 15th century velvet cope of gold woven by the women of the parish.

◎ Opposite is the Ilminster Stage, a suitable hostelry to quench parched thirsts before following another rolling road on the south side of the Culm to Hemyock.

The Culm Valley villages of Culmstock, Hemyock and Uffculme all feature in R.D. Blackmore's lesser known novel, "Perlycross".

Surrounded by hills, Hemyock has a ruined castle used as a prison by Parliamentary forces during the Civil War. In private ownership and part of Castle Farm,it is open to visitors in summer months in the afternoon. A stream separates it from the church.

◎ Wheel your bike along the path to emerge just to the right of the Catherine Wheel Pub. Turn left to find yourself at the five-road crossroads and distinctive memorial. On the corner is Brook Guest House offering accommodation, a charming tea room and a take away facility.

◎ As the main road swings left you turn right towards Churchin-ford. Cross the Madford River and bear right to climb to a crossroads at which you turn right to Madford. The lane contours the lush valley involving minimal effort.

◎ With a sense of little having changed over the centuries head for Madford and Dunkeswell Abbey turning right at the T-junc-tion to cross the river. Fork left past Musgrave Farm and take the left turn to the Abbey ruins.

The setting is enchanting and idyllic; the path to the site of the Abbey Church passes the remains of the gate-house and between two well tended gardens. The present church was built in 1842 with stones from the Abbey ruins.

◎ Leaving the Abbey site, return to the lane to Dunkeswell for a steep climb onto the ridge.

A "large" village, 800 feet up on moorland, Dunkeswell has its own church and formerly enjoyed the benefit of much Common land of which Dunkeswell Turbary remains.

**Dunkeswell Abbey ruins**

◉ Turn left at the junction above the church to drop down across the Madder and climb again. This is the Honiton road and it bears round to the right at the brow. At the crossroads turn right to head west across the old turbary. To return to Broadhembury continue across the next crossroads for a dramatic descent that brings you down to the church of St. Andrew.

◉ **To return to Whimple,** turn left just before the church heading for Hembury Fort and the A373.

If you have the energy explore the "battlements" of the most westerly Stone Age fort in Southern England.

◉ You have to turn left steeply onto the A373. The principal route takes you right at the crossroads. To view the Fort go a further 100 yards along the main road and take the footpath on the left opposite a gateway. Take care securing your bike.

Having taken in the atmosphere of this ancient camp return the same way you went up then turn right onto the A373 and return to the crossroads at which you turn left towards Talaton.

◎ A virtual two-mile descent, steep at first, takes you through Colestocks and Talewater back towards Talaton. WARNING: The A373 is a busy road especially in the summer months. It is probably safer to dismount at the crossroads and push the bike across. The descent warrants an arrow on the O.S. map and care is required – tractors and local traffic use this road.

◎ From the River Tale at Talewater there's a three-quarters of a mile climb to Bittery Cross from which you retrace your steps to Whimple.

◎ **As an equally if not more impressive route to Whimple** turn left at the crossroads where the Broadhenbury road goes ahead and down (signposted to Awliscombe) then fork right to follow a ridge that affords views of North Hill to your right, across a valley carrying a tributary of the Tale, and St. Cyres Hill to the left on the far side of the River Wolf. In early summer enjoy the aroma of freshly mown hay before plunging into the shadow of Hembury Fort to reach the A373 at a crossroads. Go straight ahead to begin the two-mile descent referred to above through Colestocks and Talewater.

# Ride 15

## *Raleigh, Recalcitrance and Rebellion*

**Route:**      West Hill – Tipton St. John – Harpford – Otterton – East
                Budleigh – Wordbury – Aylesbeare – West Hill

**Distance:**   25 miles

**Map:**        O.S. Landranger 1:50,000 Series; Sheet 192, Exeter &
                Sidmouth

---

This route follows the Otter Valley to within a couple of miles of its
outlet to the sea at Budleigh Salterton then climbs away to East
Budleigh and Hayes Barton, birthplace of Sir Walter Raleigh, traverses Common land and returns through Woodbury to Rockbeare
Hill.

◉ Begin at the National Trust Car Park on the B3180 to the north
west of West Hill (Grid Reference 063944). Turn right onto
the B road and left at the crossroads to sail down through
West Hill, bearing left at the junction beyond the small mid-
19th century church. A lovely leafy lane brings you down to
a staggered junction at which you turn right to cycle past the
Salston Manor Hotel and parallel to the River Otter which
rises in the Blackdown Hills to the north.

◉ A gently undulating lane takes you down to Tipton St. John
and over the river via a bridge constructed in 1835.

This village is Saxon in origin, "Tippa's Tun", the "St. John" being

DIRECTION
(follow the dog's nose)

MAIN ROUTE
"SIDE" ROADS
ROUTE OF OLD RAILWAY TRACK
RIVERS AND STREAMS

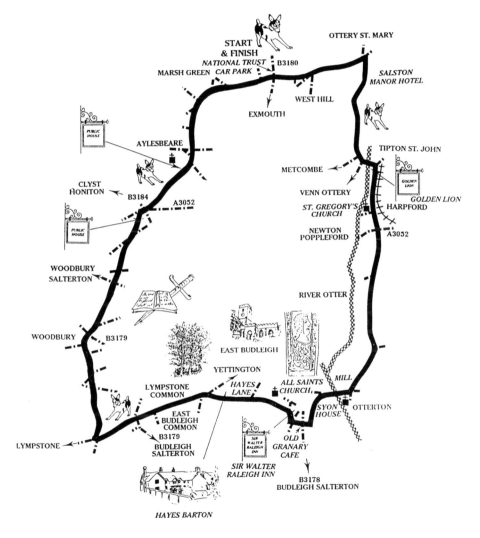

OTTERY ST. MARY

START & FINISH
*NATIONAL TRUST* B3180
MARSH GREEN *CAR PARK*

*SALSTON MANOR HOTEL*

WEST HILL

EXMOUTH

*PUBLIC HOUSE*

AYLESBEARE

TIPTON ST. JOHN

METCOMBE

*GOLDEN LION*

CLYST HONITON
B3184

A3052

VENN OTTERY

*GOLDEN LION*
*ST. GREGORY'S CHURCH* HARPFORD

*PUBLIC HOUSE*

NEWTON POPPLEFORD
A3052

WOODBURY SALTERTON

RIVER OTTER

WOODBURY
B3179

EAST BUDLEIGH

YETTINGTON

LYMPSTONE COMMON
*HAYES LANE* ALL SAINTS CHURCH MILL

EAST BUDLEIGH COMMON
B3179
BUDLEIGH SALTERTON

*SYON HOUSE* OTTERTON

LYMPSTONE
*SIR WALTER RALEIGH INN* *OLD GRANARY CAFE*

*SIR WALTER RALEIGH INN*
B3178
BUDLEIGH SALTERTON

*HAYES BARTON*

added at a later date. A late morning start might neatly coincide with opening hours at The Golden Lion.

◉ A little beyond the pub (ignoring the residential road) is a turn to the right to Harpford. Take this turn for a closer acquaintance with the river and a disused railway that used to link Feniton with Sidmouth.

Harpford's church, perched on a corner, is dedicated to St. Gregory, sharing that dedication with only four other churches in Devon. The parish of Harpford is ancient although the oldest part of the present church is 15th century. The Burial Registers record "Burials in Sheep's Wool" reflecting the 1678 Act of Parliament that ordered all burials be in wool to support the wool trade.

◉ The road now meanders through the village and past Harpford House to meet the A3052, a busy road requiring care as you turn right then immediately left to continue down the east bank of the river. A narrow lane crowded by high banks, occasionally broken to reveal the Otter's floodplain and softly rounded hills to the west, carries you to Otterton.

As you pass through the village's main street note the 300 year-old mill and bakery on the left. Otterton began as a Saxon settlement with an even more ancient settlement to the north east on the high ground towards High Peak. Alas a large ancient circle of stones was "vandalised" for use in the grotto at Bicton Park!

Harold II gave the Manor of Otterton to his mother, Gilda, who in turn granted it to the Abbot of Mont St. Michel in Normandy.

◉ After a visit to the Mill which is still in operation baking bread and mouth-watering cakes on a daily basis and where a cafe/restaurant can render the ill-disciplined cyclist reluctant to return to the saddle, you head west over the bridge and past the old station house. Take the first lane on your left and let your imagination loose.

Conjure an image of a medieval wharf buzzing with activity as wool merchants and salt producers loaded their merchandise onto ships bound for Europe and beyond. This wharf was Budley Haven and it lay within the Royal Manor of Bodeleia, a manor within the largest Hundred in the county. In 1530 the estuary began to silt up and shipping interests began to transfer elsewhere.

◎ The lane bends round to the right passing Syon House the approximate site of another monastery which was administered by the monks of Mont St. Michel.

If the name "Syon House" sounds geographically inconsistent the explanation lies in the fact that following Henry V's dissolution of all alien monasteries Henry VI ordered the revenues of the Manor lands to be paid to the House of Syon in Middlesex.

◎ The lane meets the B3178 at a crossroads which you cross to begin a gentle climb into the unspoilt and rather special village of East Budleigh. But don't miss the Old Granary Cafe on your left which proffers not only a cream tea opportunity but a host of cuddly toys. The lane through the village bends sharply right and left. The church of All Saints comes into view at the top of the street benignly overseeing the whitewashed cottages and the Sir Walter Raleigh Inn.

A Saxon Church stood on this site although most of the present building is 15th century with the exception of the 14th century porch and oak south door. The wooden pews should be examined for an illustration of life in the 16th century. The domestic life of the village in its hey day is represented by carvings of mariners, woollen themes and the like. 1537 is the date that accompanies the Raleigh coat of arms at the end of the family pew.

In 1538 a new injunction from Cromwell required the registration of all christenings, marriages and deaths with penalties for omissions. Never prone to immediate compliance with injunctions of this type the good folk of Budley treated the matter in a casual way. Similarly little heed was paid to the Parliamentary substitution of a magistrate for a clergyman to celebrate marriage (Charles II reversed this situation). The Puritans also put paid to the Ale Feasts, gala affairs involving the brewing by church wardens of ale which was then sold at the feast to raise money to support the church.

◎ Just before the church is Hayes Lane which heads west towards Hayes Barton, home of the Raleigh Family. The electricity sub-station may not be too picturesque but soon you find yourself in open farmland before corrugated roofs announce the presence of outdoor pigs and the proximity of a secluded but significant farmhouse.

**Hayes Barton**

A dwelling has existed on this site since the 13th century and at the time the Raleigh family came to occupy it ownership was with the Dukes from Dorset with whom it was to remain for 400 years. Although Walter Raleigh senior was heir to the manor of Withy-combe he chose to rent Hayes Barton from the Dukes. It was in 1552 that the afore mentioned Walter became a father to a staunch Elizabethan who would, in his early years, have played in Hayes Wood across the lane. Having served his country and sovereign and travelled widely Sir Walter Raleigh met his end on the block at the hands of James I of England.

**The tumbling weir near West Hill**

◉ Within some 50 yards or so the landscape changes quite perceptibly as you cycle through mixed woodland and emerge onto East Budleigh and Lympstone Commons. This involves some ascent but the magic of the area is such that your concentration is fixed, not on the gradient, but the vivid purple and yellow of heather and gorse flanking stands of silver birch and ash.

◉ Bear left at the next junction then, where the road forks, continue to the right. A little more climbing is required before you fall to meet the B3180. Go "straight ahead" towards Lympstone. After about half a mile of further easy pedalling there is a junction on the right. Turn right to contour farmland that manages to retain a not unduly tamed demeanour. Beyond Combe Farm go straight on at the crossroads and right at the next junction. Pass two lanes on the right and at the next junction turn right. You soon meet the B3179 at the southern end of Woodbury.

◉ As you climb gently through the village, ponder the past.

This is the area where the insurrection that followed the compulsory use of the new English prayer book was all too apparent. The Act of Uniformity, passed in 1549, required the substitution of the new prayer book for the age old mass. Many of the populace, especially in the south west, resented this and, following on from high taxes, it was not surprising that fervent opposition led to the taking up of arms. Men of high birth assumed leadership of the rebellion popularly known as the "Prayer Book Rebellion". Sir John Russell, Lord Privy Seal, was charged with quelling the uprising. His forces came up from Ottery St. Mary and West Hill and down to Woodbury. An important battle was fought near Clyst St. Mary where the back of the rebellion was broken.

◉ Go straight up through the village towards Woodbury Salterton. The road to this latter village bends sharply left but you continue straight on and up until you meet the A3052. Turn right with care and take the first left (the B3184 to Exeter Airport). Turn right almost immediately and cycle to the T-junction at the "top" end of Aylesbeare. Turn left, past the Aylesbeare Inn, and cycle through the village to a crossroads. At the crossroads go straight ahead to pick up a narrow lane to Marsh Green.

◉ At Marsh Green, you come to a junction at which you turn right (signposted Rockbeare and West Hill). A final climb rewards you with the proximity of the car park where you began your trip. To reach it, turn left at the next crossroads and almost immediately left again.

There is an interesting old mill near to West Hill with a unique 'tumbling weir' – see picture on page 99. Originally a corn mill, the weir was added in 1790 to power the new Georgian serge factory.

# Ride 16

## *Discovering the Coly and Yarty Valleys – an Exquisite East Devon Exploration*

**Route:**      Honiton to Stockland and back
**Distance:**   35 miles
**Map:**        O.S. Landranger 1:50,000 Series Sheet 192.

---

◎ If travelling solo and luck's on your side you may be able to catch the train to Honiton. If travelling in company, the option does not arise at the time of writing. Common sense may prevail in years to come (!) but in the interim, park not too far from the station.

◎ Turn right from the station or continue up New Street past the station and climb to the roundabout near the church. Bear left at the roundabout for more of the same! This gradient doesn't go on forever. Continue to a fork in the road by which time the road has levelled out and bisects the golf course. Turn right to pick up a superb ridge atop Farway Hill which bestows occasional glimpses of tumbling valleys bearing tributaries of the River Coly.

You may hit a head wind; at 250 metres or thereabouts the ridge is quite exposed. nevertheless it's difficult to detract from the pleasure of this straight level road.

◎ You cycle through conifered woodland and soon come to a junction. This is Money Acre Cross.

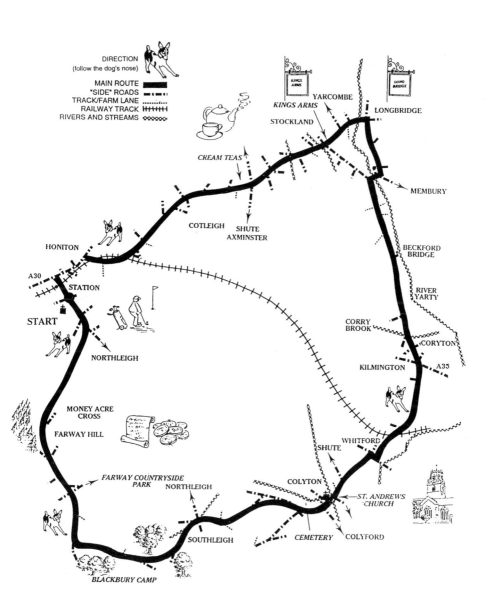

One Humphrie Hutchins discovered a cache of gold coins here together with an old parchment. As he was illiterate he took the parchment to the parson who told him he should spend the best part of the money on the repair of the church. In 1628 the church of St. Michael in Farway became the beneficiary of a new north wall and bears an appropriate inscription.

◉ Continue along the ridge and about a mile further on bear left at the junction to join the road signposted Seaton/Blackbury Camp. Cycle across the next crossroads for a gentle rise to the top of the aptly named Broad Down (234 metres). Descend and at the next junction turn left (signposted Blackbury Camp). Before long an open lane with ancient hedges (Wordsworth's "little sportive lines of wood run wild") succumbs to leafy shadows as you approach the Iron Age Hill Fort. A stroll is essential.

◉ Return to the lane and turn right to continue under the canopy to a fork. Go left for a winding steep descent into the secluded valley in which Southleigh nestles.

You may well hear the lowing of cattle before they are sighted.

◉ At the T-junction, turn right and follow the signs for Colyton.

So long as there isn't a proliferation of vehicles these lanes have, and should maintain, a timeless feel.

◉ You emerge from a close hedged lane into one of the earliest Saxon settlements in Devon down a "wide" hill, passing the cemetery on your left. St. Andrews Church tower can readily be seen and to reach it turn right at the T-junction and immediately left.

Take time to investigate the church, damaged by fire in 1933 but lovingly restored and with an imposing west window. Just above the porch is a priest's room where Colyton Grammar School had its birth in 1546.

The village boasts some delightful buildings in a picturesque but unpretentious setting and has a healthy buzz. It also houses one of the only two oak bark tanneries in Britain at Hamlyn Mills in King Street.

◎ After an amble around the village head down (with the Colcombe Castle Hotel on your left) towards the river and follow signs for Axminster and Kilmington. A steepish climb out of the valley brings you past Mounthill Farm and to Whitford.

This village supports a Methodist chapel and the tiny brick church of St. Mary's built in 1910 with seating for only 36 people.

◎ Turn right at the T-junction then take the second left passing a distinctive pink thatched cottage. Not quite apparent at this juncture but to your right is the broader Axe Valley.

The river meanders through its flood plain to Seaton and a narrow outlet to the sea.

◎ The lane goes under the picturesque Exeter to Waterloo line before climbing to Kilmington and the busy A35. Cross this with care to pick up a lane that follows the Yarty Valley. At the first junction the road bears right then bends sharply to the left following the wall of Coryton. At the next junction go right over the Corry Brook. The Yarty isn't immediately apparent but an undulating lane brings you closer as the valley narrows. About a mile and a half further on the first road on your right takes you to Beckford Bridge, an ancient monument and the oldest pack horse bridge in East Devon.

◎ Return to the lane to Stockland and after a further mile and a half turn right to cross the Yarty. When you reach a T-junction turn left.

(A right turn would take you steeply up to Membury Court, built in 1568. A Roman Villa was excavated on this site.)

◎ Stay on this road until you reach Longbridge and a pub of the same name where you can quench the thirst, restore "fuel" levels and gather your strength for the return to Honiton.

This hostelry has been serving beer for some 300 years, but once had its own sweet shop and, until recently, a blacksmith's shop.

◎ Take the Stockland road from the crossroads by the pub for a climb and a drop into a village that crossed the border from Dorset To Devon in 1842. You may wish to investigate the King's Arms for a liquid top up on a hot day. If you didn't partake of the Longbridge Arms' hospitality you would be well advised to visit this pub. It's a stiff haul up to the top of Stockland Hill. Take the Cotleigh/Honiton road out of the village.

*En route* you pass near the site of Stockland Little Castle which, along with Stockland Great Castle, was built by the Saxons as a link in a chain of fortifications against hostile attacks.

◎ The lane climbs then drops to the Corry Brook before climbing again very steeply out of the valley to meet the road that runs north-south along the top of Stockland Hill. Cross this road for a freewheel down towards Cotleigh (although you bypass the village centre) and Honiton. A cream tea opportunity arises at the farm on the right just after you begin your descent.

◎ The climbing isn't quite over. A dip towards the stream is succeeded by a rise that brings you onto a wooded ridge which takes you towards Honiton. Head into the town and the car or turn left into New Street to retrace your steps to the station.

# Ride 17

## Hidden Delights

| | |
|---|---|
| **Route:** | Farway Country Park – Southleigh – Colyton – Farway Country Park |
| **Distance:** | 20 miles |
| **Map:** | O.S. Landranger 1:50,000 Series; Sheet 192, Exeter, Sidmouth & Surrounding Area |

This route of covers part of An Exquisite East Devon Exploration and is entirely within the East Devon Area of Outstanding Natural Beauty.

◉ Begin at Farway Country Park (Grid Reference 187942) where a hundred acre Nature Reserve offers a variety of animal encounters and refreshments between Good Friday and the end of September (10 am to 6pm). Outside this season park at Blackbury Camp (Grid Reference 186924) and follow the directions from this Iron Age Fort.

◉ Leave the Country Park via the official Exit and turn right for a level-ish half mile to a crossroads at which you turn left. You pass two tumuli on your right before reaching another crossroads at which you turn left. Cycle over Broad Down, enjoying a top gear run (wind permitting) for a mile to the signposted left turn to Blackbury Camp.

◉ The lane to the camp is enchanting. Make the most of cycling on the flat as you travel along a canopied avenue. As you approach the Camp (on your right) the mixed woodland

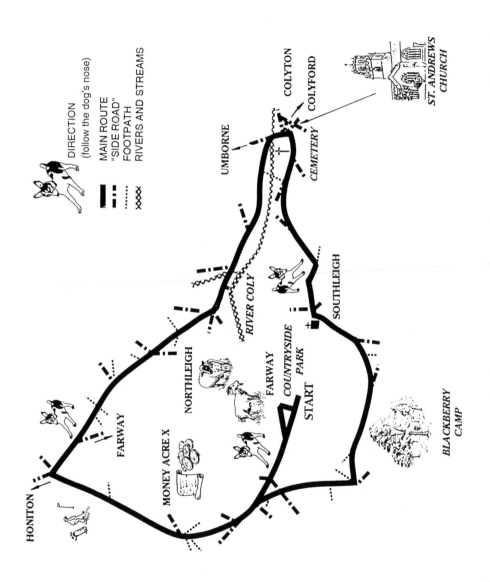

DIRECTION
(follow the dog's nose)

MAIN ROUTE
"SIDE ROAD"
FOOTPATH
RIVERS AND STREAMS

ST. ANDREWS
CHURCH

COLYTON
COLYFORD
CEMETERY

UMBORNE

RIVER COLY

SOUTHLEIGH

NORTHLEIGH

FARWAY
COUNTRYSIDE PARK
START

FARWAY

MONEY ACRE X

HONITON

BLACKBERRY
CAMP

becomes denser and, in the summer, brings welcome relief from the sun's rays.

◎ Explore the fort then return to the lane, turning right. Continue for about a quarter of a mile to a fork at which you turn left towards Southleigh. A glorious descent ensues BUT exercise extreme care after rain especially in the autumn after the leaves have fallen.

In October, when hedges have been generously trimmed, the eye is drawn to the Church of St. Lawrence nestling in the valley below and to Knowle Hill, Great Pen and Blackley Down beyond.

◎ At the bottom of the hill turn right then take the second left turn towards Colyton. After a brief rise you descend again, to a tributary of the River Coly. Follow the lane, contouring Ox Hill, to emerge at a junction where you turn left for a further descent past the cemetery.

◎ You arrive in one of Devon's oldest towns opposite Soanes Cycle Shop. Turn right then immediately left to explore this Saxon settlement, starting with St. Andrew's Church.

The town probably pre-dates the Saxons. St. Andrew's Church contains some of its original Norman fabric in the West Wall and has an unusual octagonal lantern tower. Colyton School had its origins in the room above the porch.

A number of tea shops and hostelries offer their hospitality including the Bear Inn, the Gerrard Arms, the Colcombe Castle Hotel, the Old Bakehouse Hotel & Restaurant and the Old Courthouse Tea Rooms. (This list is not exhaustive.)

◎ After exploring, find your way to the Chantry bridge that crosses the Coly just before Road Green at the eastern end of the town. (If you've become lost, return to the cycle shop and, with the lane that brought you down past the cemetery opposite, follow the road round to the right).

◎ The road climbs gently at first, with the occasional "pull".

Numerous properties are passed with the suffix "hayne" indicating a hedged enclosure.

◎ When you reach Fardown Cross turn right onto the Honiton road to begin a climb onto a ridge bestowing breathtaking views.

There's even a convenient wayside bench to sit, enjoy the tranquillity and become entranced by the higher reaches of the Coly Valley.

In Autumn the colours are outstanding. Almost immediately below you is Northleigh but a diversion necessitates a steep climb back up to this ridge.

◎ The going gets much easier as you descend to a crossroads. Go straight on and continue for about two and a half miles from the crossroads until you reach a turn on the left to Farway, just after the entrance to the Golf Club. Turn left for five miles of level pedalling if you are returning to Farway Country Park or seven and a half miles for Blackbury Camp. Both are signposted.

# Ride 18

## *Circumnavigation of the Blackdown Plateau*

**Route:**     Dunkeswell Airport – Smeatharpe – Culmhead –
               Simonsburrow – Hemyock – Dunkeswell Airport

**Distance:**  20 miles (plus 15 mile optional extension)

**Map:**       O.S. Landranger 1: 50,000 Series; Sheet 193, Taunton &
               Lyme Regis

This route from Dunkeswell Airport stays high for the most part to
form a circuit of the Blackdown Plateau and the distinctive Culmhead Beech Avenues. Busy with military air traffic in the last war,
Dunkeswell Airport is now private and home to a healthy number
of small aircraft which take advantage of the plateau at eight hundred feet.

◉ Begin in the car park at the airport (Grid Reference 138079).
The airport is open to the public and has a cafe, bar and
viewing point.

◉ Turn right from the car park towards the village of Dunkeswell
and, where the road bends sharply to the right, take the left
turn signposted "Dunkeswell Abbey". Turn immediately right
to cycle down past the Church of St. Nicholas to a junction
at which you turn left. This takes you down to the Madford
River. (* – **See note below**)

◉ Cross the river then climb sharply for a few hundred yards to
a T-junction at which you turn left. Another steep descent
brings you to Fishponds Wildlife Sanctuary, secluded in

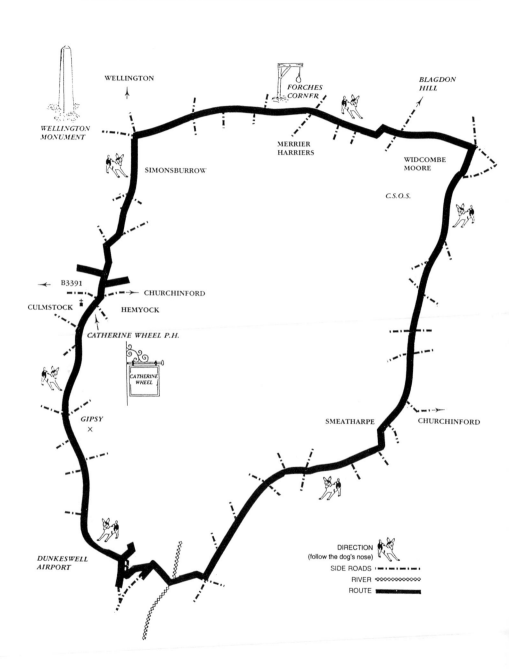

"Rough Grey Bottom". A steep pull brings you up to the road that traverses Luppitt Common. Now you can begin to enjoy miles of level pedalling.

◎ Unless the wind is unkind you sail across the Common, the Madford Valley retreating to the west, soon to pass four legged spectators at Smeatharpe Stadium. Smeatharpe today is just a scattering of buildings on either side of the road but it once boasted two inns and a turnpike gate. At the end of the village the road bears slightly left to head due north.

◎ Proceed through three sets of crossroads then begin to descend Churchstanton Hill along a beech-lined avenue that bisects one of a number of free-range piggeries that are scattered over these hills.

◎ At the junction turn left to cycle past Trickey Warren Farm and the Composite Signals Organisation Station then down over Widcombe Moor with Widcombe Wildlife Park on your right.

◎ At the crossroads turn left towards Wellington to travel along a beautiful Culmhead Beech Avenue close the point where the river Culm rises.

About two and a half miles from the crossroads you pass the Merry Harriers, boldly proclaiming the availability of "Fish and Game". Alas, this 15th century inn has been closed for some time.

◎ Continue on this ridge road, over Buckland Hill and down through the crossroads where a left turn would take you to the Half Moon at Clayhidon. A slight rise brings you to another crossroads at which you turn left to descend through Simonsburrow and Milhayes to cross the Culm and cycle gently up through Hemyock.

◎ The road swings round to the right and you come to the memorial and village pump beyond which lie Brook Guest

House and the Catherine Wheel Public House. The former provides not only accommodation but also a delightful tea room and a take-away facility.

◎ To continue take the lane between the pub and the church to wind your way up Castle Hill. The road levels out shortly after Lickam Cross. The airport is less than three miles away. Enjoy an easy cycle on this road to return to it.

**Honiton Extension**

◎ Should you feel the need for some extra exercise or if rail and your own schedule permit you might like to consider cycling out to the airport from Honiton. If so, follow the directions in the next ride "Celtic Kingdoms and Iron Age Forts" that take you to the left turn after Wolford Chapel. To continue, follow the road into Dunkeswell, climbing up from the Madford River to pass the pub on the left.

◎ Take the next turn on the right and, at the junction just ahead of you, turn right to join this route at the end of the third paragraph in the this ride **(marked with an asterisk, \*)**.

◎ To return to Honiton continue past the airport, follow the road round to the right and down over the Madford. You are retracing your steps to Honiton via the Wolford Chapel turn and Combe Raleigh.

◎ The extra distance is about 15 miles.

# Ride 19

## Celtic Kingdoms & Iron Age Forts

**Route:**     Broadhembury to Cadbury Castle and back
**Distance:**  36 miles, 45 miles or 60 miles
**Map:**       O.S. Landranger 1:50,000 Series; Sheets 191 and 192.

---

The **principal route** is from Broadhembury (about 1.5 miles from Hembury Fort) to Cadbury Castle and back. With suitable back up you might wish to cycle the linear route from Fort to Fort. Alternatively you can cycle from Honiton station to Exeter St. Davids. At the time of writing it is still necessary to book one's bike on a train and to turn up at a manned station to do so. Nevertheless it is worth the effort even though spontaneity has to give way to careful planning.

The routes and distances are: Broadhembury to Cadbury Castle Fort and back, 60 miles; Broadhembury to Cadbury Castle Fort (using cars) – 38 miles; Honiton – Hembury Fort – Cadbury Castle – Exeter St. Davids, 45 miles.

For the most of your time in the saddle you will be exploring the Terrain of the Dumnonii, the "people of the land". Their name gave rise to the present county name changing through the following forms: Dumnonia – Defaniscir (851) – Defnum – Defenum – Devon/Devonshire. These were a tribe who had come, originally, from the other side of the channel (probably Brittany). Their territory covered the greater part of Cornwall, Devon and Western Somerset (up to the River Parrett). It is thought that their tribal capital was at one time the great fortress of Hembury, an Iron Age fort superimposed on a Neolithic causewayed camp.

The Celtic kingdom of the Dumnonii continued to exist all through Romano British times and into the 10th century.

## Honiton to Hembury Fort

◎ Turn left from the station to cycle down to meet the High Street (A30) and turn right. Take the turning on the left (after about two hundred yards) which is signposted to Combe Raleigh – the road sign is on the right just beyond the church.

◎ The lane is not very wide to begin with and could be mistaken for a back road but it widens out as you descend under the dual carriageway to cross the Otter then climb past Combe Wood, owned by the National Trust.

You are following a tributary of the Otter into Combe Raleigh with Crook Hill on you right and the southern slopes of St. Cyres Hill on your left. Owned by the Raleighs in the late 13th century the village boasts an attractive 15th century church dedicated to St. Nicholas and constructed of dressed flints which come from the Greensand of the Blackdown Plateau.

◎ At the junction just beyond the church go right for a climb to a crossroads at which you turn left to join the Dunkeswell road. A steady climb brings you to a fork after a couple of miles at which you bear left towards Dunkeswell. About half a mile on you pass the lane to Wolford Chapel. The diversion to the Chapel is short and worthwhile.

◎ Having returned to the "main" road continue for a short distance to the crossroads at which you turn left to cross Dunkeswell Turbary. (See "Rivers & Ruins", ride 14) At the next crossroads turn left (signposted Awliscombe) then fork right for a glorious descent through the wooded slopes of The West Country's Finest Iron Age Fortification to meet the A373 and the Principal Route.

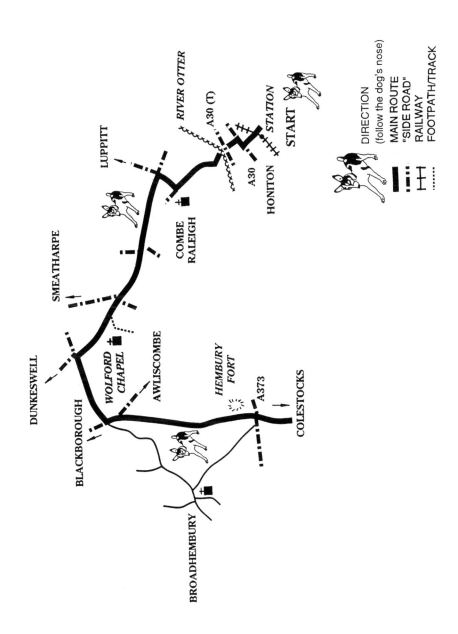

**Looking west from Hembury Fort**

## Principal Route: Boadhembury to Cadbury Castle and back

### Boadhembury to Budlake

◎ Begin in Broadhembury and cycle up past the church to take the first right turn after it for a gradual ascent to meet the A373 onto which you turn left with care.

To visit the Hillfort cycle along the main road for about a quarter of mile and you will see a footpath on the left side of the road just opposite a gateway. BE careful where you leave the bike and follow the path up immersing yourself in the ancient history that engulfs the fort and its surrounds.

◎ To return to the principal route you will have to turn right onto the A373 which can be very busy and then turn left at the crossroads for a sustained, and initially steep, descent to Colestocks.

◎ Fork left onto the road from Payhembury to reach Colestocks

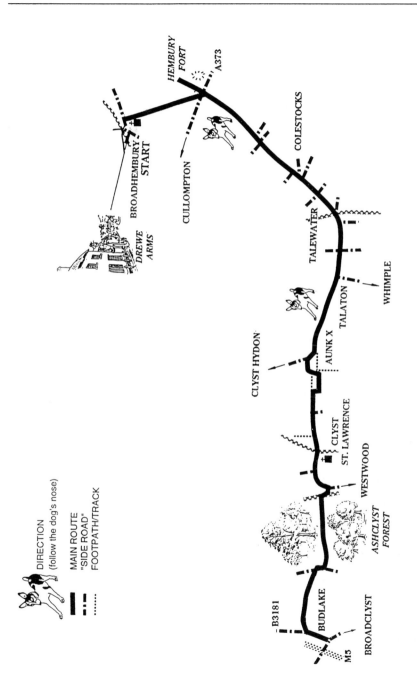

DIRECTION
(follow the dog's nose)

MAIN ROUTE
"SIDE ROAD"
FOOTPATH/TRACK

HEMBURY FORT

A373

CULLOMPTON

BROADHEMBURY
START

DREWE ARMS

COLESTOCKS

TALEWATER

WHIMPLE

TALATON

AUNK X

CLYST HYDON

CLYST ST. LAWRENCE

WESTWOOD

ASHCLYST FOREST

BUDLAKE

B3181

BROADCLYST

M5

then take a right turn to Talewater going through one cross-roads before reaching a junction at which you turn right for a three-quarters of a mile climb to Bittery Cross.

This is the site of gallows, erected to hang local followers of James, Duke of Monmouth, following his defeat at the Battle of Sedgemoor.

◉ At this crossroads go straight ahead to meet a T-junction at which you turn right. You are now in Talaton. Continue on this lane down the hill, through "parkland" until you reach the turning signposted to Clyst St. Lawrence (about a mile and a half from Talaton). Turn left. This is Aunk, a settlement with a Celtic name. Continue through Aunk (two 90 degree bends) to Clyst St. Lawrence, a settlement that gives the appearance of having changed little over the centuries and through which runs the placid River Clyst.

◉ Beyond the church you have a short climb. Ignore the right turn and follow the lane sharply round to the left for a steep descent towards Westwood but take the first right over a tributary of the Clyst and past Clapp Mill Farm. Now take the next left turn for a further climb into the lovely Ashclyst Forest, part of the parish of Broadclyst.

Don't be surprised if a deer leaps out across your path to disappear into the thickets.

◉ Shortly after a clearing on the right you reach a T-junction at which you turn right for a mile descent to Budlake and the B3181.

**Budlake via Thorverton to Cadbury and back to Thorverton**

◉ From Budlake, turn left then right on the road to Killerton, still in the Broadclyst parish.

Killerton is now mainly a late 18th century house set in fifteen acres of timbered parkland and hillside gardens. The Acland family live there having acquired the estate in Elizabethan times. However, Sir

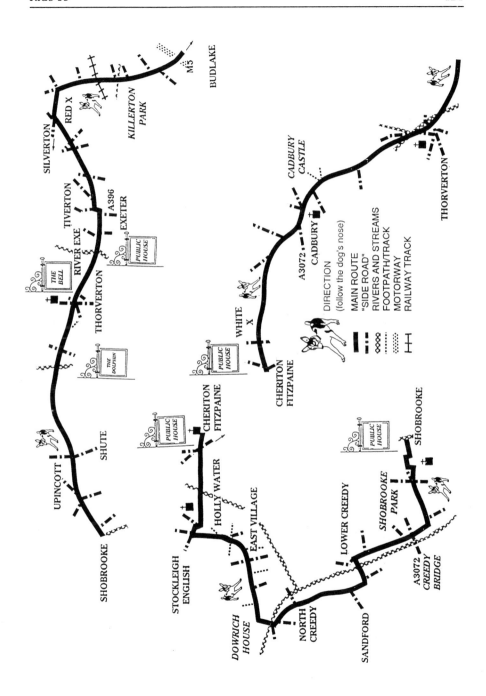

Richard Acland has handed the house and park to the National Trust. Occasional plant sales are worth patronising.

◎ Cycle alongside the park then successively over the River Culm and railway before climbing gently. Keep on this lane through a wooded cutting as it swings to the left and at the next crossroads, Red Cross, turn left for a welcome descent. Two crossroads follow in quick succession. You go through both then through the next one, Stumpy Cross soon to meet the A396. Turn left onto it then immediately right and follow this road across the Exe and up into the picturesque village of Thorverton.

This large and ancient village contains an interesting mix of cob, thatch and local stone buildings. The local stone was quarried from the 12th century onwards at Raddon, just to the south west of the village. Take time to sup at either of the two inns. The Dolphin Hotel was an 18th coaching Inn. The church of St. Thomas Becket was rebuilt in the 15th/16th century and has recently acquired two new bells to give a full complement of ten.

◎ Go up past the Post Office and at a junction demarcated by a post that has lost its "arms" turn right in the direction of Crediton. (There is a small car park just on the right.) Pass Lynch Farm on your right and then cycle through the next crossroads soon to reach Raddon Court which takes its name from the prominent range of Hills nearby ("red hill") and was a Saxon estate. Continue to a crossroads. Turn right then immediately left towards Shobrooke.

◎ This section is undulating. As you come towards the brow of the hill out of Shobrooke turn left to view Shobrooke Barton from the grounds of the church of St. Swithin which has a good Norman south doorway from about 1160. Continue up past the church to a five-lane crossroads and turn left for a descent along the southern edge of Shobrooke Park.

**Cadbury Castle**

◉ This road takes a sharp turn to the right before meeting the A3072 just to the east of Creedy Bridge which was mentioned as a landmark in a charter of 739. However, you do not go over the River Creedy. Instead turn right immediately to follow its east bank to Lower Creedy (about a mile). Turn left to cross the river and at the T-junction on the west side turn right to follow the west bank to North Creedy.

◉ Do not take the right turn over the river (unless you find yourself in need of extra gradients!) but continue round to the left to meet a lane that crosses the Creedy at Dowrich Bridge. Yet another "short sharp climb"is required then the lane bends sharply to the right where a lane leads to Dowrich House on the left, the home of the family of the same name from about 1200 until 1717. Follow this lane to Stockleigh English through East Village. This requires a right turn at the crossroads at the brow of the next hill.

◉ Follow the lane round to the right (passing the church on your left) and drop down to the Holly Water. Momentum gained as you cross the stream may carry you part way up the hill to Cheriton Fitzpaine.

The name of the village means "churchtown" and indicates a church in pre-Conquest times. The church of St. Matthew is entirely a 15th century building.

◉ Continue through Cheriton Fitzpaine and straight through the crossroads at White Cross then follow this lane until you meet the A 3072. Turn left and then turn right with care to Cadbury (not to be confused with North and South Cadbury in Somerset). Cycle past the church and after about a quarter of a mile there is a footpath on the left. The road continues round to the right.

◉ To visit the site of the Iron Age Fort, take the footpath (having secured your bike as best you can).

◎ After enjoying truly splendid views from the 829ft iron age earthwork return to the lane and continue downhill to Thorverton.

### Thorverton to Broadhembury

◎ From Thorverton retrace your steps to cross the Exe but at the next crossroads turn left towards Up Exe and the A396. Turn left onto the A road then take the first right turn to Silverton, one of Devon's oldest villages dating from the first years of the Saxon occupation.

The church of St. Mary, mostly a 15th to early 16th century building, is constructed of the local volcanic stone.

◎ As you come into the village you arrive at a small roundabout. Turn right. After about three-quarters of a mile you reach Red Cross (where you previously took a turn to meet the A396). Go straight on then take the second turn on the left to Bradninch. In the next two mile stretch you do enjoy some easy pedalling but there are also some short sharp slopes.

◎ When you reach a crossroads (High Hill Cross), turn left into the village. After the White Lion on your left the road steepens to bring you into the village centre. If you did not opt for the real ale selection at the White Lion try the Burtons or Dartmoor Ale at the Castle Inn. Both pubs do good food.

◎ To continue, return towards the White Lion and take the left turn towards Hele for a freewheel with views of the forested slopes which you encountered earlier. As you drop towards the River Culm the road bends sharply to the left then runs across the railway and under the M5 to emerge at a junction with the B3181. Turn left and then almost immediately right. Beware of fast traffic on this "straight".

◎ The lane onto which you have turned climbs gradually. If cycling in late September or October the hedges will be

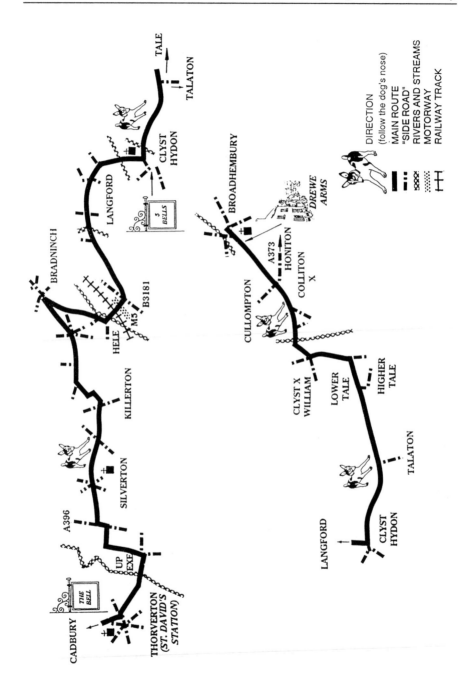

uniformly cut to afford extensive views over the Culm Valley back to Bradninch and beyond and north west towards Cullompton.

Down on the slopes just below you a herd of red deer (heading for the dinner table?) can be seen browsing.

◎ This is a particularly kind stretch of road that continues as you approach Newcourt Barton at Langford where it bears right before meeting a junction.

◎ Turn right towards Clyst Hydon and cycle through this long linear village. On the far (eastern) edge of the village is the Post Office. Less than half a mile from this the road swings sharply to the right. You, however, go straight on towards Tale.

◎ There are in fact two Tales, Higher and Lower. Enjoy a mile . that begins on the level then climbs very gently. When you come to a T-junction turn left for a dip and a climb through Lower Tale. At the crossroads turn left. At the next crossroads (Clyst William Cross) turn right towards Payhembury, passing Danes Mill and crossing the River Tale. The lane bends to the right to meet a T-junction at which you turn left to cycle up to the A373 at Colliton Cross. Go straight on and follow the lane back into Broadhembury.

**Thorveton to Exeter St. Davids**

◎ You will return to Thorverton, passing the church on your right and arriving at a crossroads with the Dolphin Hotel opposite you. Turn right to cycle familiar territory up past the Post Office. Instead of taking the right turn which you took earlier in the day go straight on to Raddon and at the T-junction turn left to head due south. The terrain is undulating but not arduous. About a mile after crossing a small tributary of the Exe you come to a staggered crossroads. Go straight on and

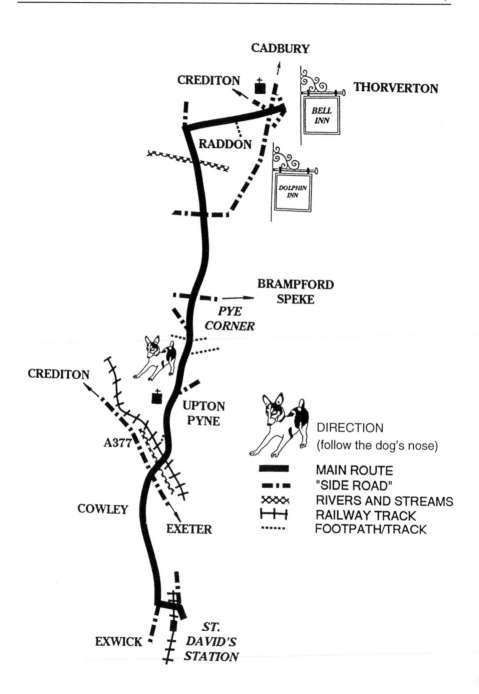

**CADBURY**

**CREDITON**

**THORVERTON**

BELL INN

**RADDON**

DOLPHIN INN

**BRAMPFORD SPEKE**

*PYE CORNER*

**CREDITON**

**UPTON PYNE**

**A377**

**COWLEY**

**EXETER**

**EXWICK**

*ST. DAVID'S STATION*

DIRECTION
(follow the dog's nose)

MAIN ROUTE
"SIDE ROAD"
RIVERS AND STREAMS
RAILWAY TRACK
FOOTPATH/TRACK

at the next crossroads straight on again. At Pye Corner go straight on towards Upton Pyne. This involves the last serious climb of the day.

The church of St. Mary is built of the local volcanic stone and has a particularly beautiful tower, with figures of the four Evangelists at the corners and that of Christ in Benediction on its West face. The chancel has some 14th century work. Fine views are to be enjoyed from the churchyard.

◉ At the end of the village take the road towards Exeter and Cowley. Descend to cross the railway and river before turning left onto the A377. Take the next right turn to continue south on the west bank of the Exe towards Exewick. As you come into the built up area turn left to cross the Exe, cycle across the railway and at the main road turn right to follow signs to St. David's Station.

**St Mary's 12th-century church, Honeychurch (ride 21)**

# Mid Devon

# Ride 20

## *The Three Rivers Route – Lowman, Exe and Batherm*

**Route:**    Shillingford to Tiverton and back by Bampton

**Distance:**  25 miles

**Map:**      O.S. Landranger 1:50,000 Series; Sheet 181, Minehead & the Brendon Hills

---

This route takes as its theme the Rivers Lowman, Batherm and Exe. For a Devon route, the contours are uncommonly kind, at least for the first half!

◉ Start from the Barleycorn Inn in Shillingford (Grid reference 982240). Turn right onto the B3227 towards Bampton. The road follows the River Batherm. Take the second turn on the left (about three-quarters of a mile on) towards Huntsham. You begin to follow a tributary of the Lowman River. A steady climb is required. Nevertheless, in Spring the banks of wild flowers – violets, stitchwort, dog's mercury, yellow archangel, celandine, primrose, forget-me-nots – create a distraction from the effort.

◉ Just past Dowhills Farm the road levels off before descending to Huntsham. A diversion into the village takes you to the hexagonal post office (a former toll house?) Return to the road junction and take the Uplowman lane following the Lowman which meanders under it.

Inescapable at times is the unmistakable aroma of wild garlic. If

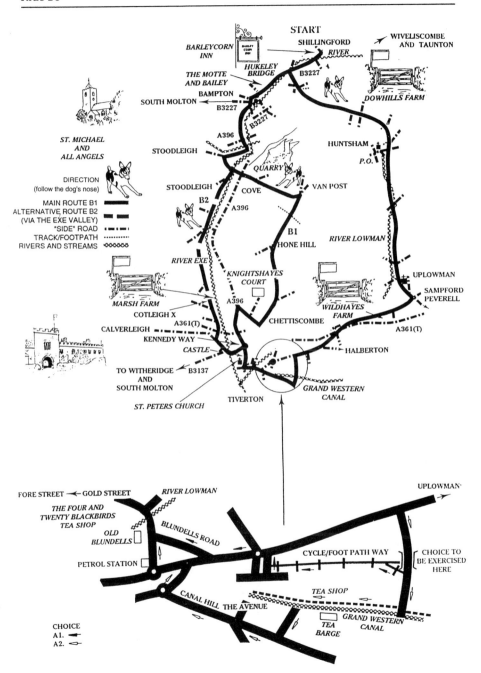

more than three or four cars have passed you by this stage the road is busy!

◎ The road swings round to the left into Uplowman some four miles or so from Huntsham. Pass the 19th century church on your left and cycle up to the crossroads. Turn right for a level couple of miles passing Wildhayes Farm on the left and Bradford Farm on the right. Follow the lane over the busy A361(T) until you hit a T-junction. Turn right and take the second road on the left, past the school playing fields. You now have a choice:

◎ **Option 1.** At the bridge (about 350 yards from the left turn) stop and carry your bike down the steps on the far side to pick up the cycle/footpath that follows the disused railway line into Tiverton. This may be enjoyed for about half a mile. At the end the cycle path emerges onto an area of grass. Turn right along the footpath and then left onto the road. At the roundabout ignore the side road on the left and go straight ahead then take the first turn on the right. This is Blundells Road. Follow it to the T-junction.

(No tea shop on this option but you can save yourself for the tea room at the bottom end of town and it's worth it)

OR

◎ **Option 2.** Cross the bridge over the cycle/footpath and drop down to a bridge over the Grand Western Canal. Turn right onto the tow-path and WALK the bike for about a mile.

A variety of water-fowl may be seen including the occasional water rail emerging from the waterside undergrowth of grasses and rushes. More common are mallards, teals, pintails, coots and moorhens. Two refreshment opportunities present themselves:

From April onwards refreshments are available either from the tea barge (originally used to transport limestone, the canal is now a restored recreational route) or the tea shop which displays, on the outside wall of a thatched cottage, a collection of over 20 teapots.

An excellent selection of teas is on offer in addition to goodies to satisfy hunger pangs.

◎ Having quenched thirsts, go to the end of the access lane and turn right with care onto Canal Hill. The road layout has recently changed. Follow the road round to the right to meet the new Relief Road onto which you turn left. At the round-about turn right passing a petrol station on your left. Continue down past Old Blundells.

The routes have now converged.

Now privately owned by the National Trust, Old Blundells was originally founded in 1604 as a free grammar school by Peter Blundell who made his future in the manufacture of Tiverton "Kerseys".

◎ Keep left and cross the River Lowman by the Lowman Bridge to come up Gold Street.

Mid Devon District Council produces an excellent "Tiverton Town Trail" which is worth following if time permits. Walking your bike through the town (recent pedestrianisation measures prevent cycling through the town) will guarantee seeing several of the Trail's features. (Old Blundells and The Lowman Bridge are two of them) These include the Greenway Almshouses and Chapel on the left side of Gold Street.

◎ Continue up Fore Street, then bear right up St. Peter Street past Slees or Widow's Almshouses and The Great House of St. George, a Jacobean mansion.

A visit to St. Peter's Church will reveal some glorious stonework.

◎ Back on the bike now to head up Park Hill past the Castle. You are again presented with a choice:

◎ **Option 1.** Cross the next two roundabouts and proceed, following the signs, to Knightshayes Court. This National Trust property comprises a rare survival of the work of Victorian Architect William Burges and a garden noted as one of Devon's finest. Visit the garden in Spring to appreciate the full carpet of wildflowers under the cultivars.

◉ To continue, return to the entrance/exit and turn left then left again before the A361 to wind your way up to Chettiscombe. Bear left at the fork to follow the course of Town Leat north (a stream running along the right side of the lane but not often visible). A two mile climb ensues through the forested Hone Hill. As you emerge from the woods the road gets even steeper: there's no shame in dismounting; the author does! About two miles further on you come to a crossroads, Van Post, where a left turn reveals fabulous views of the fringes of Exmoor. Now comes the real pay off for your efforts – a sustained steep descent into Cove. **Make sure those brakes are in perfect order.**

◉ At the A396 go straight on at the staggered crossroads to drop more gently to the bridge over the Exe, an ideal resting point. If you have rested the momentum to carry you part way up will have been lost. Never mind. Push or pedal the bike up the hill after crossing the bridge.

OR

◉ **Option 2.** To enjoy a closer relationship with the River Exe, turn left at the first roundabout onto Kennedy Way which crosses the Exe. Take the first right turn (to Rackenford) and continue on this road for about half a mile. Take the first right turn downhill to cross the A361(T) and follow the Exe Valley Way. At the first junction go right to follow the lane to Cotleigh Cross. Turn right (signposted Lower Washfield and Cove). You will know by now that following the Exe Valley involves some sharp inclines and declines! Pass Marsh Farm and go right at the next junction. The lane now weaves along the edge of woodland inhabited by buzzards with another sharp short hill. At the next junction, Newbridge Cross, turn left in the direction of Stoodleigh. Ignore the next two left turns to

Stoodleigh soon to arrive at a junction where a right turn brings you to Cove Bridge and a small thatched cottage. This is an excellent spot to take a break but lost momentum almost guarantees walking the bike back up the hill.

◎ The routes have now converged.

◎ Stay on the west side of the river and go straight up from the cottage.

◎ This road rises to pass a rather stark new dwelling which contrasts sharply with the richness of the surrounding woodland with its abundant flora. Turn right at the junction to cycle along the top of the now defunct quarry which was evident from the east side of the valley. Drop down to the bridge over the river and cross the A396 for a further slope to pick up the River Batherm. As you approach the village of Bampton follow the road up to the junction with the B3227. Turn right onto this B road which runs through the village and eastwards to Shillingford, the Barleycorn and beyond.

**Bampton**

This village of Celtic and Saxon origin is well worth exploring. The church, dedicated to St. Michael and All Angels, dates in part from the late 12th century but it occupies the site of a Saxon wooden one built in the early 8th century. The Swan Hotel, near the church, dates from 1450 and was built to house the Master Craftsmen who were enlarging the church. It now serves a fine pint of Cotleigh Tawny Bitter!

Many of the houses in the town centre were built of stone from the town quarries in the 18th century by wealthy wool merchants, the finest example being Leburn House in Luke Street.

The Motte and Bailey on the edge of the village, and suitable for a visit on the way back to Shillingford, is the site of a wooden fortification built around 1086.

"A Short History of Bampton, Devon" by T.J. Francis at £1.35 is available from the Tourist Information Office in Brook Street.

# Ride 21

## *A Mid Devon Meander*

**Route:**     Exeter – Hatherleigh by "Bike Bus" and back
**Distance:**  31 miles
**Maps:**      O.S. Landranger 1:50,000 Series; Sheets 191 and 192

---

Devon County Council is sufficiently far-sighted to have introduced a Bike Bus, equipped to carry six bicycles. This special service (No. 361) runs daily from Exeter to Barnstaple and back during the summer months (see Appendix I, Bikes 'n' Buses). A cross-country route is designed to enable an appreciation of Devon's glorious countryside. The "parkland that characterises the Exe Valley gives way to the rolling hills of Mid Devon before you travel along the northern edge of Dartmoor gaining views of the highest tors on the Moor.

◉ This route requires you to disembark at the bus stop in the Market Place in Hatherleigh (just before the Spar shop).

Given that you are dropped off at the lower end of town the scope for temptation before you get going is ample. Acorns Tea Rooms is succeeded by the 15th century George Hotel which boasts the date of its construction underneath a thatched roof. If you have not yet been allured, the Tally Ho Inn on the right of the main street, with its own brewery, beckons. Beyond and on the left, adjacent to the Antique shop on the corner of the Square, the aroma of freshly baked apple muffins assails the nostrils and tempts you into the Tea Room.

Opposite is Elizabeth Aylmer's Pottery, well worth a visit but perhaps better left to another day unless you feel the need for some extra ballast.

## Hatherleigh to Coleford

◎ At the top of the town, where the main A396 bends sharply to the left, you take the right turn down an unsigned lane. This road dips briefly before climbing to a junction. Turn left (towards Monkokehampton) to cycle past the monument on the left and begin to take in the splendour of the North Dartmoor Tors to your right.

Beyond Okehampton and the A30 rise Yes Tor and High Willhayes Tor, at over 2000 feet the highest point on Dartmoor. Devoid of tree cover the Moor's rugged beauty can be transformed into a brooding wilderness with the temporary disappearance of sunlight. You can see the weather coming in from miles away.

You are pedalling through an area that has been settled for centuries. Below Deckport Cross lies Deckport Farm, an Elizabethan house and Upcott, a farmstead on an ancient site. Another ancient site is Velliford, off to your left as you descend towards Monkokehampton.

◎ Descend to cross the River Okement before meeting the B3217 at Monkokehampton, Turn left then immediately right down the lane that is signposted to Broadwoodkelly.

(The hamlet takes its suffix from the Kellys who held the manor from the 14th century.)

◎ Cycle upwards but not for too long to find yourself on another ridge with fine views of further tors.

Immediately to the south are Row Tor, Scarey Tor and Belstone Tor. The easternmost high point is probably Cosdon Beacon.

◎ Take the third turn on the left towards Bondleigh and cross Taylor's Down to meet the B3219 at a crossroads. Go straight on to enjoy a descent to Bondleigh, situated in the Upper Taw Valley.

A short diversion to the left at the first crossroads will take you to the Norman Church of St. James, rebuilt in the late 15th and early 16th centuries.

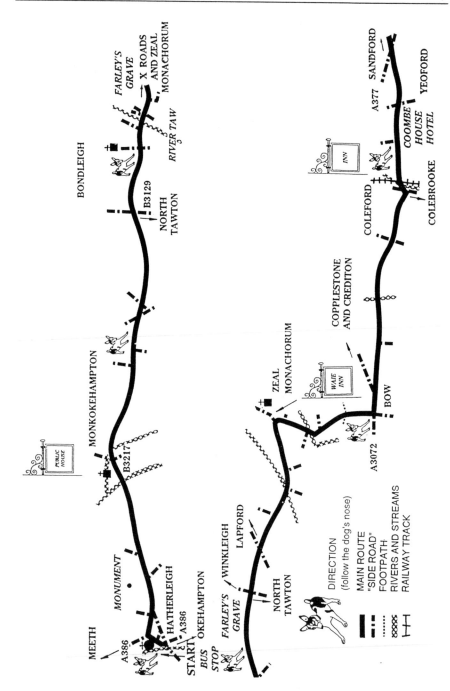

MEETH

MONUMENT

A386

A386

HATHERLEIGH

A386

OKEHAMPTON

BUS STOP

START

PUBLIC HOUSE

MONKOKEHAMPTON

B3217

BONDLEIGH

B3129

NORTH TAWTON

FARLEY'S GRAVE

X ROADS AND ZEAL MONACHORUM

RIVER TAW

FARLEY'S GRAVE

WINKLEIGH

LAPFORD

NORTH TAWTON

ZEAL MONACHORUM

WAIE INN

COPPLESTONE AND CREDITON

BOW

A3072

COLEFORD

INN

COLEBROOKE

COOMBE HOUSE HOTEL

COLEBROOKE

A377 SANDFORD

YEOFORD

DIRECTION
(follow the dog's nose)

MAIN ROUTE

"SIDE ROAD"

FOOTPATH

RIVERS AND STREAMS

RAILWAY TRACK

◎ Continue downhill to cross the Taw and climb towards Lowton. The gradient eases as you climb towards the crossroads at Farley's Grave. (I've yet to discover who the unfortunate Farley was.) Go straight on in the direction of Zeal Monochorum.

◎ At the next crossroads cycle straight over, descending to meet and cross the stream called Gissage Lake. Follow this lane for just over a mile to find yourself in the village of Zeal Monochorum. When you reach the T-junction opposite the church turn right for a sharp drop.

◎ On the left, after about a hundred yards is a sign to the Waie Inn.

If in need of a break or refreshment, turn left at the sign to find the pub and sports centre.

◎ To continue follow the lane down towards the River Yeo. The bridge makes a pleasant al fresco snack point but you can bet that in this region, oft described as "unfrequented", what little traffic there is will suddenly become concentrated on this spot.

◎ A stop at the bridge will deprive you of the momentum to climb the ensuing hill, but the gradient isn't too unkind. Sutton Farm is at the brow after which there's a compensatory drop before a sharp short pull brings you to the A377 at Bow. Turn left onto the main road and, after half a mile, take the right turn to Coleford and Colebrooke.

Bow is a large street village on the Crediton-Okehampton road which once held a weekly market granted in 1295 and, at the feast of St. Martin, a three day fair. The main street was the obvious place to site the market and fair and that was how Bow was born. The parish, however, was centred on Nymet Tracey. "Nymet" signifies a sacred or consecrated place or grove (from "nemeton") where the Celts would have worshipped their gods.

◉ Enjoy the next three and a half miles to Coleford. You cycle along another ridge (with a few gradients) of a different character from those on the north side of the A30. Although you cycle through fewer pockets of woodland, to the south are the tree clad combes between and aside tributaries of the River Yeo.

◉ Drop down to the delightful village of Coleford deep in country settled for centuries.

**Coleford to Exeter**

Whelmstone Barton to the west is an ancient freehold estate first recorded in 1249 but probably older.

◉ Go straight on at the crossroads to climb and regain the height just lost. A mile further on you pass Coombe House now used as an hotel. Continue to meet the A377. Turn right then immediately left towards Sandford.

This lane traverses Chapel Downs on the north of Crediton and maintains an exquisite panorama of Devon hills. Although not as thriving as it once was, Crediton has an important place in the region's history. Prior to being removed to Exeter Crediton was the episcopal base for the Diocese of Cornwall and Devon. The Pope at that time – 1050 AD – considered Crediton a mere "villula" (hamlet). Exeter was a more fitting location for the regional religious centre. Before the transfer of the Holy See, nine bishops had ruled from Crediton.

Crediton thrived when the woollen industry was at its height. Decay set in with the coming of the railway in the mid-19th century.

◉ Continue on the Sandford lane until you come to a crossroads. Go straight ahead to skirt the southern edge of Creedy Park. Cycle straight on at the next crossroads then left at the following junction to meet the A3072 after two hundred yards or so. Turn left onto the A road then take the first right after

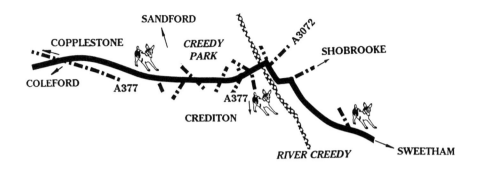

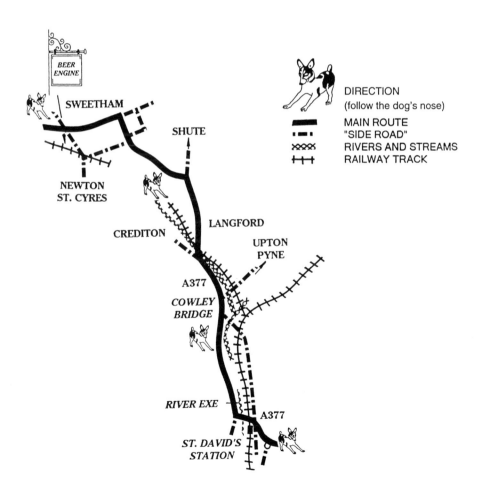

crossing Creedy Bridge (mentioned as a landmark in a charter of 739) towards Shobrooke.

◎ This road follows the southern bounds of Shobrooke Park. Just as an impending hill might bring dismay you turn right for a further descent along the north bank of the River Creedy in the direction of Newton St. Cyres. At the next crossroads turn right towards Sweetham and the renowned Beer Engine Pub. *En route,* you pass a garden with a highway signpost in it.

◎ From Sweetham, (the group of dwellings in the vicinity of the pub), do NOT cross the railway line but cycle straight on and at the next two junctions turn right. The second of these will bring you into Langford, on a rise. Continue over the railway to meet the A377. Turn left to brave this busy road for half a mile.

◎ Just over the brow of the hill, and beyond the pub on your right, is a right turn. Take this lane towards Exwick (there's a small church on the left just as you begin to cycle down the lane).

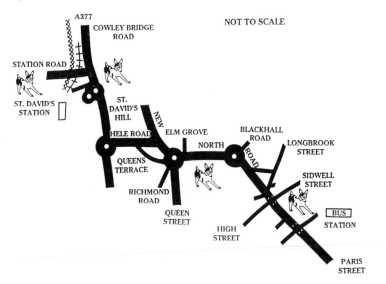

◉ Continue in "rural mode" for just over a mile to a junction at which you turn left to cross the Exe and the railway line immediately north of St. David's Station. When you met the A377 again turn right WITH CARE to cycle across the roundabout up St. David's Hill. At the next roundabout turn left along Hele Road. From here follow the directions on the plan for the City Centre to the Bus Station (and from there to your car).

# Appendix I – Public Transport

## Bikes 'n' Buses

In 1994, Devon County Council and Devon General Ltd introduced the Bike Bus. Specially adapted to carry six bikes, secured at the rear, the bus ran in August and September on a daily basis (excluding Wednesdays) from Exeter to Barnstaple. Apart from the passenger fare there was a flat rate of £2 for bicycles. It was operated on a first-come-first-served basis with no pre-booking.

It is intended to run the service again in 1995 from the end of May through to the end of September. For further information telephone Barnstaple/Exeter/Torquay 382800.

A cross country route provides the opportunity to explore the Tarka and Sticklepath Cycle Trails or to 'pioneer' your own trail.

## Bikes 'n' Trains

No innovations here! Over recent years provision for cyclists in the south west have diminished. A leaflet is published by Travel & Marketing Company on behalf of Regional Railways entitled, 'Cycling by Train'. It is available from your local station. There is no uniformity across the country so be sure to check the position. At the time of writing the Exeter-Waterloo Line carries only one bicycle per train so the prospect of cycling with the family or friends and using the line is somewhat limited!

The position on the Paddington – South-West line is rather better as Inter City trains can carry up to three bikes.

It is not possible to reserve spaces over the telephone.

The facilities for carrying bicycles change from time to time and the leaflet covers the same periods that Railway timetables cover i.e. the end of September to the end of May and the end of May to the end of September.

## Private Railways

The West Somerset Steam Railway's 'old' rolling stock, for its steam and diesel services, lends itself to the carriage of bicycles. Old style guards' vans and courteous staff make cycling in conjunction with train travel a joy.

# APPENDIX II – Tourist Information

The Tourist Information Centres that are located within the region comprising this 'West Country' are listed below.

**Somerset:**
Bridgwater
50, High Street
Tel: 01278 427652

Burnham on Sea
South Esplanade
Tel: 01278 787852

Chard
The Guildhall
Fore Street
Tel: 01460 67463

Cheddar
The Gorge
Tel: 01934 744071

Glastonbury
The Tribunal
Tel: 014458 832954

Minehead
17, Friday Street
Tel: 01643 702624

**Devon:**
Axminster
The Old Courthouse
Church Street
Tel: 01297 34386

Budleigh Salterton
Fore Street
Tel: 01395 445275

Crediton
Market Street Car Park
Market Street
Tel: 01363 772006

Exeter
Civic Centre
Paris Street
Tel: 01392 265700

Exeter Services
Devon TIC
Sandygate
Tel: 01392 437581

Honiton
Dowell Street Car Park
Tel: 01404 43716

Podimore
Somerset Visitor Centre
Forte Services
A303, Nr. Yeovil
Tel: 01935 841302

Okehampton
3, West Street
Tel: 01837 53020

Sedgemoor Services
Somerset Visitor Centre
M5 South, Nr. Axbridge
Tel: 01934 750833

Ottery St. Mary
The Flexton
Tel: 01404 813964

Taunton
The Library
Corporation Street
Tel: 01823 274785

Seaton
The Esplanade
Tel: 01297 21660/21689

Wells
Town Hall
Market Place
Tel: 01749 672552

Sidmouth
Ham Lane
Tel: 01395 516441

Yeovil
Petters House
Petter's Way
Tel: 01935 71279

Tiverton
Phoenix Lane
Tel: 01884 255827

Tiverton Services
Junction 27 (M5)
Nr. Sampford Peverell
Tel: 01884 821242

Apart from information on places to stay, to eat and to visit, the Information Centres will have up to date information on Cycle Hire and the increasing number of Cycle Trails which the Local Authorities are promoting.

# APPENDIX III:
# Cycle Hire & Other Recommended Routes

## Cycle Hire

Both Somerset and Devon County Councils, through their Tourist Information Centres, can provide detailed information about regional and locally available cycle hire facilities.

Devon County Council produces a booklet entitled, 'Walking & Cycling in Devon' which is available at the Tourist Information Centres (at a modest 50 pence in 1994). This contains a list of cycle hire establishments in the county. The following is not a complete list and no responsibility is taken nor any recommendation made:

## Devon

### Exeter

**Saddles and Paddles**, The Quay, Exeter. Tel: 01392 832062 – open all year.

**Flash Gordon**, Prestons Yard, Ludwell Lane, Exeter, EX4 2AQ. Tel: 01392 213141/78041/411880/433435.

Honiton
**Cycle Honiton**, Lanson House, King Street, Honiton EX14 8AA. Tel: 01404 47211 – open all year.

Tiverton
**Maynards Cycle Shop**, 25 Gold Street, Tiverton, EX16 6QB. Tel: 01884 253979 – open all year.

## Somerset

### Taunton

**Ralph Coleman Cycles**, 79 Station Road, Taunton. Tel: 01823
275822 – open all year.

### Langport

**Frank's Auto Needs & Cycles**, North Street, Langport, TA10 9RQ.
Tel: 01458 250348

# Other Recommended Routes

## Devon

The 'Walking and Cycling in Devon' publication lists a number of
designated routes across the county ranging in distance from two
miles (Ilfracombe to Motenhoe through a nature reserve) to thirty
miles (Sticklepath Cycle Route).

## Somerset

The County Council has produced a series of routes concentrated
on the area of the Somerset Levels and Moors. These, together with
the South Somerset Cycle Route (now also marked up on the
relevant O.S. 1:50,000 Landranger Series), are available from Tourist
Information Centres.

# Appendix Iv – Favourite Fuel Stops

The following list is of pubs, tea rooms and other refreshment stops not specifically referred to in the Route descriptions but in their general vicinity and which I have found to be well worth a visit. A cheerful welcome awaits and all diets and palates are catered for although my particular preference is for vegetarian and fish dishes.

## Devon

### Public Houses and Inns

The Otter Inn, Weston, Nr. Honiton; Tel: Honiton 42594; excellent menu with children catered for; real ales.
Jack-In-The-Green, Rockbeare; Tel: Whimple 822240
The Ring of Bells, Cheriton Fitzpaine; Tel: Cheriton Fitzpaine 866374
The Prince of Wales, Holcombe Rogus; Tel: Greenham 672070; excellent Ales and a local Stout from Ashburton.

### Tea Rooms and Restaurants

Pophams Bakery, Castle Street, Winkleigh; Tel: Winkleigh 83767. Imaginative and extensive variety of dishes produced for the discerning palate served in the daytime only. Booking for lunch is highly recommended as the 'Bakery' only holds nine people. Morning coffee and the temptation of truly wicked desserts alone could render the cyclist reluctant to return to the saddle!
Jolly's, The Bank, Newton Poppleford; Tel: Sidmouth 568100. Restaurant open from 7pm Tuesday through to Saturday. NB: In the winter, the restaurant is only open from Tuesday to Thursday if there are advance bookings; it is always open on Fridays and

Saturdays. Excellent selection of inspired vegetarian cuisine at reasonable prices. Carnivores also catered for.

A La Ronde, Summer Lane, Exmouth; Tel: Exmouth 265514. This National Trust sixteen-sided house has a Tea Room open during the general opening hours of the House: 11am – 5.30pm from 30th March to 30th October.

# Somerset

## Public Houses and Inns

The Burtle Inn, Catcott Road, Burtle; Tel: Chilton Polden 722269; excellent selection of food including a children's menu; wide selection of real ales.

The Old Pound Inn, Aller; Tel: Langport 250469

The Ring O' Bells, Pitt Hill Lane, Moorlynch; Tel: Ashcott 210358

The Rising Sun, Lower Knapp, North Curry; Tel: North Curry 490436; Country Pub and award winning restaurant specialising in seafood. Associate Member of 'Taste of the West' – see note below.

The George Inn, 42 Main Road, Middlezoy; Tel: Burrowbridge 698215). Unspoiled village pub with long-standing reputation for excellent ales.

The Frog and Slate, 22 Silver Street, Ilminster; Tel: Ilminster 52741). The menu is biased in favour of the carnivore but this is a friendly hostelry where you should ask for the explanation behind the proliferation of amphibian accoutrements.

The Greyhound Inn, Staple Fitzpaine; Tel: Hatch Beauchamp 480227). Good food, ale and a variety of live music.

The Queen's Arms, Pitminster; Tel: Blagdon Hill 529.

The Martlett, Langford Budville; Tel: Milverton 400262

## Tea Rooms and Restaurants

The Goat House Inn, Bristol Road, Brent Knoll; Tel: Brent Knoll 760995. A flock of English goats are kept here. Their products, chiefly cheese, milk and yoghurt are available.

The Old Bakery, Kingston St. Mary; Tel: Kingston St. Mary 45205.

Morning Coffee and Cream teas in a picturesque Somerset village with a particularly fine church tower.

East Lydeard Farm, Bishops Lydeard, Taunton; Tel: Taunton 432668. Cream teas on offer at a mixed farm which also grows and sells soft fruit. Winner of several Conservation Awards.

Number 10, 10 Station Road, Taunton; Tel: Taunton 246045. Vegetarian, vegan and organic dishes available from the cafe or the retail bakery.

## Notes

(1) 'Taste of the West' is an organisation promoting the array of quality food and drink produced in the West Country.

(2) Times of opening vary so it is advisable to check before turning up at the above establishments. I have been caught out, especially on Mondays!

(3) The longer list for Somerset is merely a reflection of my greater familiarity with that county's eating establishments and hostelries. My exploration of Devon's is very much ongoing.

# Appendix V – O.S. Maps Covering The Region

**O.S. 1:50,000 Landranger Series:**

181 Minehead & Brendon Hills area

182 Weston-Super-Mare & Bridgwater area

191 Okehampton & North Dartmoor area

192 Exeter, Sidmouth & surrounding area

193 Taunton & Lyme Regis

# Bibliography

You will find scores of books on the West Country in Tourist Information Centres and Bookshops. However, those listed below have proved a consistently good read and encouraged me to delve further into the background of the Region.

**Avalon & Sedgemoor** by Desmond Hawkins (Published by Tabb House Ltd.)

**Exe to Axe** by Gerald Gosling (Published by Alan Sutton Publishing Limited)

**The Devon and Somerset Blackdowns** by Ronald Webber (Published by Robert Hale & Company). This book is now out of print but can be obtained through the library.

**The Origins of Somerset** by Michael Costen (Published by Manchester University Press)

**Quantock Country** by Berta Lawrence (Published by Somerset County Library)

**Somerset Curiosities** by Enid Blyford (Published by Dovecote Press)

**Somerset Places & Legends** by Ray Gibbs (Published by Llanerch Publishers)

We publish guides to individual towns, plus books on walking and cycling in the great out-
doors throughout England and Wales. This is a recent selection:

## More Books from Sigma about the South-West!

CORNISH PLACE NAMES AND LANGUAGE – Craig Weatherhill *(£6.95)*

MYTHS AND LEGENDS OF CORNWALL – Craig Weatherhill & Paul Devereux
*(£6.95)*

EXPLORE THE COAST OF DEVON – Paul Wreyford *(£6.95)*

BEST PUB WALKS IN NORTH DEVON – Dennis Needham *(£6.95(*

PUB WALKS IN SOUTH DEVON – Laurence Main *(£6.95)*

PUB WALKS ON DARTMOOR – Laurence Main *(£6.95)*

PUB WALKS IN CORNWALL – Laurence Main *(£6.95)*

## Lots more Cycling Books too!

CYCLE UK! The essential guide to leisure cycling – Les Lumsdon *(£9.95)*

CYCLING IN THE SCOTLAND & N.E. ENGLAND – Philip Routledge *(£7.95)*

OFF-BEAT CYCLING IN THE PEAK DISTRICT – Clive Smith *(£6.95)*

MORE OFF-BEAT CYCLING IN THE PEAK DISTRICT – Clive Smith *(£6.95)*

50 BEST CYCLE RIDES IN CHESHIRE – edited by Graham Beech *(£7.95)*

CYCLING IN THE COTSWOLDS – Stephen Hill *(£6.95)*

**CYCLING IN THE CHILTERNS** – Henry Tindell *(£7.95)*

**CYCLING IN OXFORDSHIRE** – Susan Dunne *(£7.95)*

**CYCLING IN THE LAKE DISTRICT** – John Wood *(£7.95)*

**CYCLING IN LINCOLNSHIRE** – Penny & Bill Howe *(£7.95)*

**CYCLING IN NOTTINGHAMSHIRE** – Penny & Bill Howe *(£7.95)*

**CYCLING IN SOUTH WALES** – Rosemary Evans *(£7.95)*

**CYCLING IN & AROUND MANCHESTER** – Les Lumsdon *(£7.95)* .. *available 1996*

**CYCLING IN STAFFORDSHIRE** – Linda Wain *(£7.95)* .. *available 1996*

**CYCLING IN NORTH WALES** – Philip Routledge *(£7.95)* ... *available 1996*

## *Even Football and Golf ...*

**RED FEVER: from Rochdale to Rio as 'United' supporters** – Steve Donoghue
*(£7.95)*

**UNITED WE STOOD: unofficial history of the Ferguson years** – Richard Kurt
*(£6.95)*

**MANCHESTER CITY: Moments to Remember** – John Creighton *(£9.95)*

**MANCHESTER CITY: an A to Z** – Dean Hayes *(£6.95)*

**GOLF COURSES OF CHESHIRE** – Mark Rowlinson *(£9.95)*

- plus many more entertaining and educational books being regularly added to our list.
All of our books are available from your local bookshop. In case of difficulty, or to obtain our complete catalogue, please contact:

**Sigma Leisure, 1 South Oak Lane, Wilmslow, Cheshire SK9 6AR**
**Phone: 01625 – 531035          Fax: 01625 – 536800**

ACCESS and VISA orders welcome – call our friendly sales staff or use our 24 hour Answerphone service! Most orders are despatched on the day we receive your order – you could be enjoying our books in just a couple of days. Please add £2 p&p to all orders.